ORADOUR-SUR-GLANE

A VISION OF HORROR

Guy PAUCHOU
Sub-prefect of Rochechouart

Dr Pierre MASFRAND
Curator of the ruins
of Oradour-sur-Glane

A VISION OF HORROR

OFFICIAL PUBLICATION
of the Remembrance Committee
and the National Association of the Families of the Martyrs
of Oradour-sur-Glane

2003 EDITION

ASSOCIATION NATIONALE DES FAMILLES
DES MARTYRS D'ORADOUR-SUR-GLANE.

Note to readers

The National Association of the Families of the Martyrs of Oradour-sur-Glane has accepted the generous gift of labour from the authors of this work.

M. Guy Pauchou, former Sub-prefect of Rochechouart and Doctor Pierre Masfrand, First Curator of the village of martyrs of Oradour-sur-Glane. They express their enormous thanks to them.

This volume, edited by the National Association of the Families of the Martyrs of Oradour-sur-Glane, is a collection of witness statements taken in the days following the drama.

It is a contribution of respect and to the memory of the martyrs of Oradour.

On this tenth day of July, 1945
the Court of Rochechouart pronounced
that those whose names are included in the list at the back
of this work, being all victims of the 10th June, 1944,
should carry in the register the inscription :

« Died for France »

FOREWORD

Apart from one bare mountain where life seems to labour arduously to make headway, Limousin is simply full of harmonious countryside, cool clearings, deep ravines and gentle undulations.

Everywhere, from spring to the first day of autumn, an undefinable, « local » green spreads out in triumph. Whether it colours the grasslands watered by the Vienne or the imposing woods along the Uzerche road with its bends so tight that you always imagine starting them over again, it's a green that has perhaps learnt its secret from the numerous springs that abound everywhere.

A traveller in june 1944 leaving Limoges for Angoulême would have been captivated by the charming balance of the surrounding countryside. How easily he would have stepped aside from the main road to take some more intimate by-way to discover to his delight, above the meandering river Glane, between two rows of willows and poplars, the church of the town going by the melodic name of Oradour.

A few days later, nothing was left of this village apart from ruins and embers, the blackened sections of walls grasping the sky like stumps, and the charred remains of its inhabitants. The Huns had been that way, killing, pillaging, destroying, burning and anihilating animate beings and inanimate alike with method and refinement, for in the art of killing they are masters « par excellence ».

The various episodes in this tragedy have been reconstructed by Monsieur Guy Pauchou, sub-prefect of Rochechouart and Doctor Pierre Masfrand, curator of the ruins of Oradour in an accurate and detailed work in which the simple account of the facts witnesses, far more than any commentary, of the hateful crime, one among many, of the occupier.

The day before, ninety-nine hostages were hanged at Tulle ; the day after, forty eight were to be killed by the firing squad at Mussidan ; for several months already, an angry thirst for blood had been given free reign in the area. It was horror raised to the level of a political policy with the aim of terrorising French people aligned against the invader and who were preparing to achieve their own liberation by their own means.

These were crimes of no purpose and empty effort for the resistance would never give in to such abominable blackmail. The treacherous cruelty of the adversary would, on the other hand, exalt their patriotism, strengthen their will, inflate their desire for revenge and lead them to victory.

Hitler would have had trouble for nothing ; the German people would be left with their innocent corpses, their futile murders, their indelible shame and their dishonour established once for all.

And nothing will ever wipe out from the consciousness of mankind the memory of Oradour, which symbolises the barbarity of a people that from its number recruited the assassins.

Pierre BOURSICOT
Commissioner of the Republic

The crime is signed… yes, it is signed : Hitler !

It is premeditated crime, coldly prepared and systematically executed…

Its purpose : by means of fear to subjugate the masses of our people and to prevent them from gaining their freedom.

But it was in vain !

All that is left of the Boches'invention is an irremovable shame for Germany.

But that shame thrusts back onto those who are unworthy to be called French and who collaborated with these so-called bearers of civilisation.

CHAINTRON
Prefect of Haute-Vienne

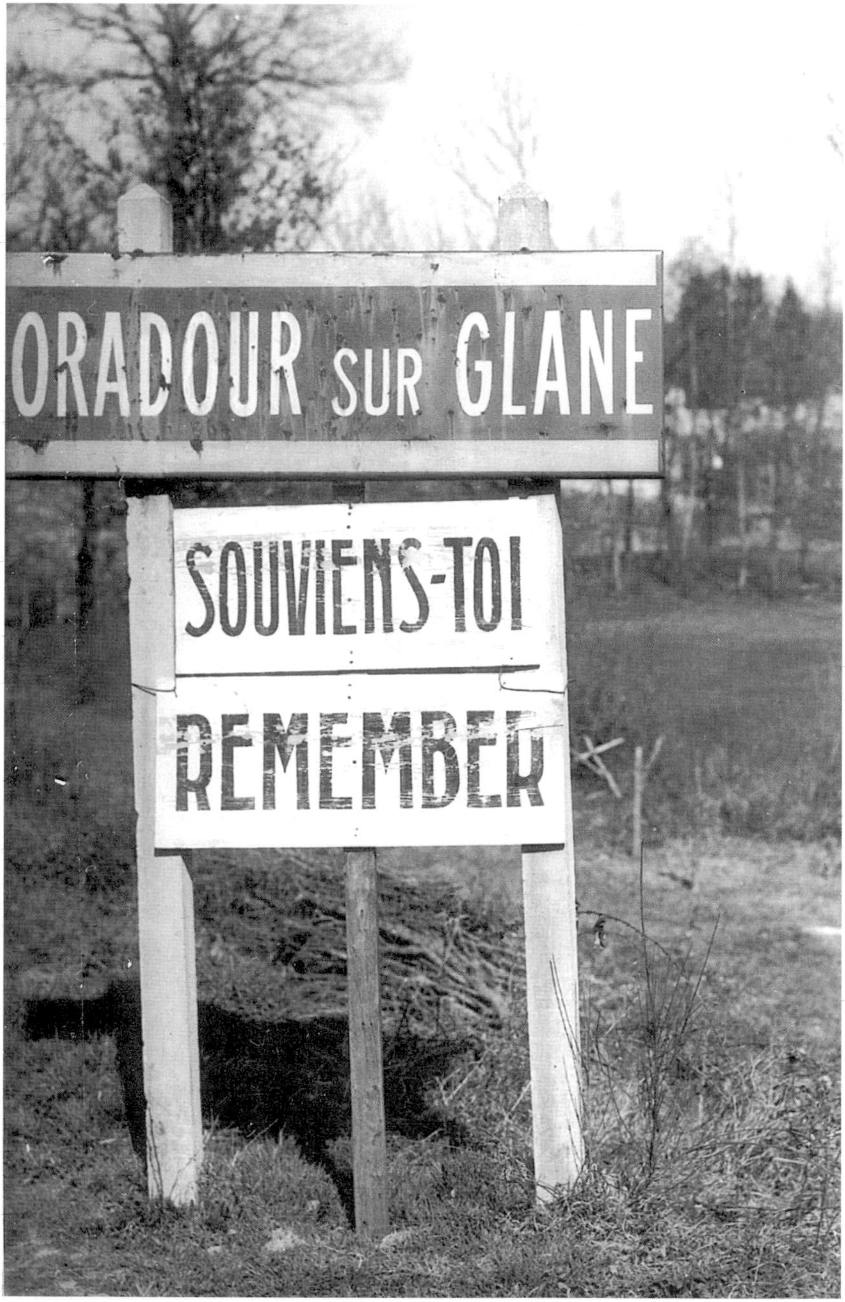
ORADOUR SUR GLANE
SOUVIENS-TOI
REMEMBER

THE EPISODE

The town of Oradour

Oradour-sur-Glane, crucified with such atrocity by German bar-barity, was a charming, attractive, small town of Limousin in the area of greater Rochechouart. According to the 1936 census, its population was 1,574, including 330 in the town itself. At the time of the action, bearing in mind many refugees who were there, the latter figure was certainly double.

It was pleasantly situated on the banks of the Glane, a pictu-resque river which Corot discovered the previous century, devoting several noteworthy to it which achieved world-wide renown. The banks of the river, supposedly haunted by muses wearing barbi-chets, the local head-dress, were the inspiration of numerous poets who never ceased extolling its intimate and penetrating charm. The river runs through a restful and agreeable setting, singing under deep green cradles its eternal hymn of glory to our beautiful Limousin.

The town was clean and tastefully built, with a diversity of modern, well-to-do shops. Its life went on quietly under the shade of its old church. Although this building suffered enormously during the fire and the roof and woodwork completely disappeared, the architecture of the stonework largely escaped from the disaster. The church is very old and, as we shall see, is of as much interest from an aesthetic viewpoint as archeologically. The nave and the side chapels date from the fifteenth century. The left side chapel has a superb rib vault resting on four sculptured consoles representing famous people.

Entrance to the town and church before the fire.

One of these, the *chabretaire*, or musette player, is very interesting and has often been described and depicted elsewhere. The fortified bell tower dates from the sixteenth century and is shored up by two high, stark buttresses surmounted by two kinds of bartizans.

The name of Oradour, which comes from the Latin *oratorium*, indicates that from the Roman period there was an *oratorium* there. i.e. an altar and a place to offer prayers for the dead, who at that time were buried along the roadside or in the vicinity of crossroads.

Oradour certainly lived up to its destiny !

Alas, it could never have better deserved the name it received !

A lantern for the dead is erected in the middle of the cemetery which is classified by the administration *des Beaux Arts* and mentioned in all the archeological works on the Limousin. This type of monument is fairly sparse. So few have withstood the test of time.

*
**

The Countryside around Oradour is rich and fertile. The region is agricultural, its foremost specialisation being in animal breeding. That is why, during the war, its inhabitants had the advantage of an unusually large food supply. Those of the neighbouring townships would often come there for supplies.

Several reputable hotels shared the numerous and pleasant clientele of this small centre - Hotel Milord, especially known for its good cuisine had a large number of long term tenants including many well-off refugees who had come to seek asylum in a happy region that they thought sheltered from all danger.

Many city dwellers met there for business purposes or even just to forget the restrictions and discipline of the war whilst the shaded banks of the *Glane* were host to crowds of anglers immersing themselves in their favourite sport.

It was into this small, quiet, delightful town that the German hordes would perpetrate perhaps the most monstrous and abominable crime in our history.

S.S. billeted around Oradour the night before the massacre

It has been established that the perpetrators of the action belonged to the famous S.S. « der Führer » regiment. On the 20th August a broadcast from Radio-London informed us that the unit which had committed the atrocities of Oradour-sur-Glane had been identified. Radio-France had just announced that it was the 3rd company of the S.S. « der Führer » regiment which was part of the 2nd Panzer division known as « das reich ». We will show the result of our research on this subject in a later chapter. It has been established that an inhabitant of the area surrounding Oradour, in whose house these soldiers had, during their tragic expedition, left certain parts of their uniforms, had removed from the back of one of them the figure 144. This may be nothing more than a roll number. Perhaps a simpler explanation is that we are witnessing an error due to the German stylisation of the two letters S.S. which, as is well known, looks very similar overall to the figure 44. By including a more of less straight mark to its left it could be taken for the number mentioned.

A detachment of this division was billetted on the 9th June in the area bordering Oradour : one part at Rochechouart, the other at Saint-Junien. Reproduced opposite is a pass which is in our possession, issued and signed by an officer of the Saint-Junien contingent. This document contains nothing that might identify this group. After so many threats of retribution that allied Radio had addressed to troops who contravene the laws of war, it is easy to realise the utility of such a precaution.

The detatchment left in Rochechouart conducted itself with the utmost barbarity, M. Raymond Proust, mayor of the town at the time, told us :

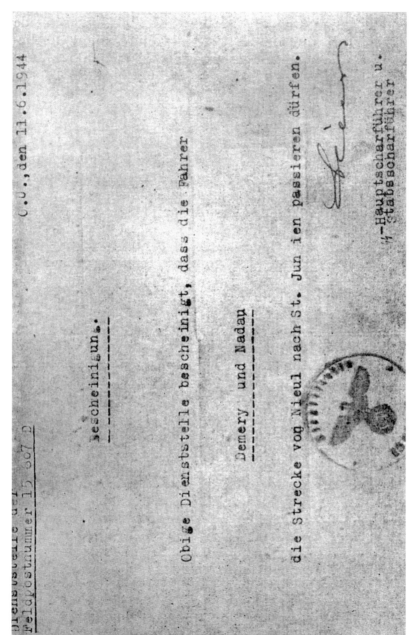

Dienststelle der
Feldpostnummer 15 607 D   O.U., den 11.6.1944

Bescheinigung.

Obige Dienststelle bescheinigt, dass die Fahrer

Demery und Nadau
----

die Strecke von Nieul nach St. Jun ien passieren dürfen.

ϟϟ-Hauptscharführer u.
Stabsscharführer

Fac-simile of a pass.

« On the 9th June at 8.30 a.m. I learnt from the sub-prefect of Rochechouart that the head of a detachment of Germans had arrived at Saint-Junien and had just telephoned from his office to see if a unit to be billetted at Rochechouart had arrived. I arranged for the figitives from the Compulsory Labour Office and the young men of the township to be immediately alerted to give them time to leave the town.

« At about 9.30, two S.S. men, their bayonettes extended, came to fetch me at the Town Hall and brutally made me follow them. I felt that I was being arrested. I was led to the command post of the unit commander and brought before him. He was a young officer of about 25, tall, thin and blue-eyed ; I would recognize him again if I saw him face to face He demanded an immediate plan of locality. Afterwards he questioned me for some time about « terrorists » that may have been in the region. I emphatically denied there were any.

« The S.S. then helped themselves to the best cars in the town, smashing garage doors and beating owners who did not obey their orders quickly enough with great brutality.

« During the night they made numerous visits to people's homes in which they committed despicable acts.

« On the morning of the 10th June at about 6 o'clock M. Paynaud, a worker, while scything near his home, was shot and seriously injured. His father-in-law, M. Fredon, was arrested along with a young man of his family. Both were beaten to make them admit the existence of « terrorists » at Rochechouart. Both kept silence heroically.

« During the afternoon, the S.S. posted sentries along the terrace of the Promenade des Allées which overlooks the country from an impressive height. From there they opened fire on locals (men and women) passing peacefully by on the roads or working in the fields. Mme Brousse from Chabeaudie, aged 67, who was just on her way back from shopping in town, was killed. I then went to the command post of the S.S. captain to protest strongly against the gunning. The officer answered dryly « There is no more firing ».

But at the same time other shots were going off. A young woman, Mme Duchambon, as she was cycling by, and my housemaid, a Spanish refugee, as she was travelling to Babaudus, were injured in their turn.

« The troop contingent that arrived at Rochechouart the first day was directed that same evening to Saint-Junien.

« Since the unit that operated at Oradour came from This town, there is every reason to believe that part of the forces from Rochechouart participated in the massacre.

« It might be useful in this respect to question some S.S. members originating from Schiltigheim (Alsace) who spoke fluent French and where being used as interpreters. They were known at Rochechouart where they had stayed at the beginning of the war. These troops gave the locals impression that they were trying to stir up incidents that they could use as an excuse to carry out reprisals, however the population did not react as they wished but instead remained calm and the troops left hurriedly after the carnage of Oradour during the night of the 10th to 11th June not forgetting to utter the severest threats of death and fire.

« They seemed particularly trained in this method of occupation.

« They said they had seen action in Russia and came from the Ukraine. One soldier said incidentally that their unit had been billetted previously in Valence-d'Agen ».

It should be noted that during the afternoon of the 10th June, a section of the detachment billetted at Rochechouart travelled to the small industrial zone of Saillat, roughed up the people there and assassinated a worker for the crime of being from Lorraine. One particularly evocative incident occurred when the officer in charge of the « expedition » became angry with the factory director, calling him a *capitalist*, then, turning against a worker, punched him sneeringly for being a *communist*.

View of Milord hotel before the fire.

That fateful day

There were rarely as many people in Oradour-sur-Glane as there were on that Saturday, on the 10th June, 1944. Quite apart from those inhabitants who were too busy at work in the fields to leave the area and the usual refugees, which included evacuated children from the South, especially from Nice, Avignon, Montpellier and Bordeaux, numbers in the town were increased by other coincidental factors.

A medical visit had filled the school building with children. Furthermore, there was to be a tobacco distribution at the town so there were plenty of tobacco lovers there, mostly farmers from the surrounding region. When one considers that some week-end trippers had arrived for rest or for provisions, it is apparent that the little town centre was quite a lively place on that day.

2 p.m. — Lunch had just ended ; people eat later in the country especially when work in the fields is at its height. The hotels were crowded.

Hotel Avril was brim full of guests. Amongst them, let us mention a lady, her three children and grand-niece fleeing from the danger of bombardments in Paris, a veterinary captain from Reims, his wife and nephew, a woman from Montpellier with her mother, a Bordeaux family, father and two children, one or two Jewish families hiding under assumed names, an old lady from Rennes and a family from Limoges.

As it was a Saturday, there were more clients passing through than on other days. The tables were full.

Mme Avril, remembered as a particularly friendly and active hostess, was making final preparations for the meal.

At Milord hotel, lunch had just been served. It had drizzled in the morning but was becoming brighter ; news of the recent Normandy landings was excellent. About twenty were sitting at table. The menu looked promising.

Amongst the regulars were Parisians with their families, people from Limoges, a champion chistera player from Marseille and a young lady who had come just to arrange transport for her valuables and silver from her home. Some lodgers had only arrived at the hotel the previous night whilst one couple had left there that same morning ! Who can fathom doom's allotment ? There was chatting and mirth ; mention was made of two customers passing through who the day before had mystified those on the top table by asking some rather personal questions and putting pressure for answers on those sitting with them.

While everyone was starting lunch, two trainee school teachers twenty years old (one attached to the school of Oradour, the other to a school in a small local village), took their meal early and left the dining room before the others to be in time for their lessons. The one from Oradour accompanied her friend along the road leading to her village school ; after greeting traders standing chatting in their doorways, they parted with what was their last farewell.

We might mention that a group of about twenty students from Limoges teacher training college had decided to take advantage of their friends being in Oradour to make a lunch excursion, on that very day ; but at the last moment the trip had to be cancelled. Once more the call of destiny !

There were a number of schools at Oradour with many children in attendance, boys as well as girls and M. Pont, the primary inspector of Rochechouart, the schools administrative centre, gave us the following testimony :

« There were two school groupings at Oradour, the boys school opposite the tram station, with headmaster M. Rousseau and deputy headmistress Mme Rousseau. The girls school had three classes, two in the town centre and one on Peyrillac road consisting of an infant section. The headmistress was Mme Binet, who was away sick and being replaced at the time by a young stand-in, Mlle Couty. Mlle Bardet and Mme Vincent were deputy heads.

« Since the war a special school for refugee children from Alsace-Lorraine had been created which was led by a local teacher, M. Goujon.

A view from the town before the fire. The schoolchildren.

« On the day of the action there were therefore two male and five female teachers at Oradour-sur-Glane, none of whom escaped the massacre.

It would seem from the registers that this school centre was quite large :

> Boys school : 64 pupils registered,
> Girls school (3 classes) : 104 pupils registered,
> Alsace-Lorraine school (1 class) : 21 pupils registered,
> **Total :** 191 pupils registered.

The Germans arrive

2.15 p.m. — We asked some of those who escaped from the tragedy to recount to us the arrival of the S.S. in Oradour. These were bold young people who managed to throw off the pitiful destiny of their compatriots, sometimes in the most dangerous circumstances (which shall be recounted later).

It was M. Hubert Désourteaux, the son of the Chairman of the special Delegation, who first observed the initial onsurge of the Nazis into the village whilst lying low in his home :

« All of a sudden », he told us, « the people of the village were seized with agitation. A heavy lorry convoy was coming in along the Limoges road and holding up in the lower part of the town. They were transporting a large S.S. detachment that could be estimated at about two hundred strong. They were helmeted and wore large jackets of thick, flecked waterproof cloth coloured mostly green and yellow.

« There were ten or so vehicles, five of which (three lorries and two half-tracks) moved through the main street, rue Emile-Désourteaux, making for the upper town, where they stopped. Almost straightaway, the two trackers came back on the side of the church and some German soldiers got out of their vehicles. What did they want ? We were soon to find out ».

Emile Désourteaux's street before the fire.

Another escapee, M. Clément Broussaudier, 26, testified :

« On the 10th June, 1944, after the arrival of the Germans in the town of Oradour-sur-Glane, Depierrefiche, the town crier, went through the streets reading out an order requesting all inhabitants, without exception, men, women and children to assemble immediately at the Market Square with their papers for an identity check ».

M. Darthout, another survivor of the incident added :

« The S.S. who had got out of their vehicles went into houses in Oradour, had every door opened and, under threat of arms, brutally forced everybody, even the ill, to go to the assembly point ».

M. Broussaudier explained :

« Mme Binet, a school teacher, was ill in bed but was forced, despite her condition, to get up and out. I saw her on the Market Square in her pyjamas with her coat on. All the houses in the village were visited carefully one after the other. »

M. Armand Senon, 29, also an escapee, witnesses that his crippled uncle was beaten and also made to leave. Mme Lang and her husband were hidden behind a window in Mme Raynaud's bedroom and were also present at the start of the drama.

« The Krauts », Mme Lang told us, « came brusquely into the open houses, guarded any exits made the people get out towards the town center under pretext of checking their papers. Two S.S. men pushed our gate, banged repeatedly at the door and shouted « Monsieur, Monsieur » in their German accents. The banging increased. Father Lorich, a priest from Lorraine, was living in a wing of the house. I heard him answer « A minute, a minute, we're coming ! » He opening his door and they swiftly grabbed him without leaving time for him to get his hat, then they took his sister, a lady friend visiting from a neighbouring village and three children ; they then made them move towards the town centre ».

Every testimony confirmed that these troops proceeded without hesitation, methodically and with order, just as if on manœuvres. Mlle Maria Gauthier, 17, of Place de La Motte in Limoges, even testified that a command post had been set up in a building along the Bordes road belonging to M. Thomas, a baker.

The schoolchildren

The schools weren't overlooked either but were invaded almost simultaneously by the Germans, who assembled the children, both boys and girls, and made them get ready to leave. As far as concerns the boys school, several unverifiable stories were told to the effect that upon arrival of the Nazi troops, the headmaster, M. Rousseau, tried to get his pupils to flee but the detachment head intervened, advising that a skirmish was expected to take place in the village and that he would himself escort the children to the church to « assure their safety ».

Some even tell that to get the schoolchildren to follow them more easily, they offered them sweets or, as some say, a photograph session, such that the classes of two hundred or so kids, their teachers in the lead, were directed by their executioners to leave in relative calm and without even a worry.

But what difference does it make what reason they were given ? What is certain is that they all left the school and that not one of them returned from that tragic walk.

With, however, one exception : a young schoolboy from Lorraine by the name of Roger Godfrin who warned one of his little friends : « They're Germans, I know what they're like. They'll try to hurt us. I'm going to try and escape ». He did indeed escape through the garden behind the school, hid among the clumps of greenery and disappeared in the woods. He was found by others from Lorraine the day after in the village of Laplaud.

The Market Square before the fire.

Assembling of townsfolk
At the Market Square

The man hunt

The « collection » of poor little schoolchildren was taking place at the same time as the collection of the rest of the inhabitants of Oradour.

The testimonies to follow establish that one by one or in groups, escorted and overseen by the S.S., everyone came together at the Market Square. But the Germans were not happy just to assemble those living in the village itself ; they went to get people in their very homes from neighbouring villages.

M. Joyeux, 53, who was near the village of Bordes, gave the following precise account of the matter :

« Immediately after the Germans arrived, there was a considerable movement of lorries in the region. As soon as they arrived, some vehicles took up positions in the surrounding countryside. This was noticed more or less everywhere especially in the area around the village of Bordes, behind the cemetery, at « Les Brégères » and at « Puygaillard ».

« Soldiers armed with automatic weapons and rifles got out and surrounded the area, forcing anyone they found along the road or in the fields back to the market Square. S.S. men wandered in the fields and hid behind hedges to surprise those who tried to escape. Farmers had to leave their work. Shots rattled out. Several people were brought down ».

Amongst these we mention Messieurs Foussat, Villoutreix, Michel Avril, Lachaud and others about whose deaths we shall say more later.

Another witness, M. Darthout confirmed :

« I was at the assembly. Small lorries were continually bringing in people from the surrounding villages and there were also some farmers from « Les Brandes » and « Bellevue ».

« The lorries would disappear then return each time with new

The main street before the fire.

The main street after the fire.

contingents of unfortunates on their way to their fateful destiny. Amongst them I recognized M. Dupic coming in from Bordes ».

2.45 p.m. — « All the inhabitants of Oradour », M. Darthout continued, « finished assembling at the village square, women in tears or some more confident or courageous, some carrying babies in their arms or pushing men who seemingly had just got out of bed. Men were there too, some interrupted right in the middle of work, like the baker, bare-chested and covered in flour.

« Prominent people were there also : Doctor Désourteaux senior, chairman of the special Delegation, then the notary, M. Montazeaud, the chemist, the boys school headmaster, M. Rousseau, and his family ; there were traders, artisans and refugees from neighbouring villages, all with their families, down to the last person. School children were there too with their teachers ».

Mme Lang, hidden, as has been said, behind her window, saw this deplorable, mournful column of unfortunates making their way to the Market Square.

« What an anguishing sight », she said, « of mothers enfolding their babies in their arms and others pushing them in prams. Young girls were crying. Then the schoolchildren arrived, boys and girls, making their way to their place of execution. I can still hear the sound of those poor kid's shoes tapping the road, overshadowed by the heavy thud of their torturer's boots.

« Suddenly, Doctor Jacques Désourteaux, the mayor's son, after finishing his round, arrived back in his car. He parked not far from the assembly point. A German went up to meet him and ordered him to join his fellow citizens ».

Doctor Désourteaux senior, Chairman of the special Delegation was quickly beckoned by an officer : « Get me thirty hostages ! » he said brutally. The mayor, with great dignity, replied that it was impossible for him to agree to this request. He was taken to the Town Hall where he remained a short while and then returned to the assembly point. He was overheard saying to the officer that he would select himself and that if further hostages were required then they only had to take his family.

M. Darthout added :

« During that time we were surrounded by German soldiers and six sub-machine guns were trained on us. Each gunner was in position with his assistant. I felt that at the least attempt to escape we would be brought down. We stayed like that until about 3 o'clock.

3 p.m. — « When the entire population was together », M. Darthout continued, « the Germans divided them into two groups, one comprising the women and children, one the men ».

« The first group, guarded by eight to ten S.S. men and including the children from the schools, was directed at about 3 p.m. to the church. There were definitely more than two hundred of us on the square. The S.S. counted us then arranged us in three rows and made us sit down and wait on the kerb, facing the wall.

« I then risked a glance behind me in spite of the order and I saw the group of our mothers and ladies, pitiful as they got further away. Women were crying, others were fainting. They were holding each other up. I saw... for the last time my wife, in tears, disappearing with the others as they turned the corner.

« They had to find a pretext for the terrible massacre they were preparing. An interpreter stood forward and announced « there are secret arms and munitions deposits here made by « terrorists ». We shall make searches. During this time, to facilitate our operations we shall put you in the barns. If you know of any such deposits », he added, « we request you to reveal them to us now ».

« M. Lamaud remarked : « I have a 6 mm. Carbine which has authorisation from the council ». The German replied : « That's of no interest to us ».

« No one admitted to any deposit and for the good reason that there were none. It was a totally peaceful village where each went

The Market Square where the assembly of inhabitants took place.

about his own small business or farming his land. I must mention that never was any assassination committed against any German soldier and there was no reason that might justify the least reprisal from them.

3.30 p.m. — « A few moments later », M. Darthout continued, « the Germans split us into a certain number of groups which they escorted, machine guns in hand and with great brutality, force and threats, to various points in the village ».

M. Armand Senon confirmed this account. He was 29 years old. As he was incapacitated by a broken leg from playing football, he could witness the assembling from the first floor window of his house situated at the Market Square. He could see the comings and going of lorries and gun cars. « My mother », he said, « came up to the room where I was and explained that the whole population hat to meet at the village square for an identity card check. My parents had tried to escape but they were brought back to the Market Square along with my grandmother, my aunt and uncle. None of them came back.

« At that time, he added, « I saw men sitting in three rows along the Market Square guarded by German soldiers armed with machine guns and rifles. Suddenly an officer, tall and thin looking, came from the side of the church to speak to M. Désourteaux. After a short discussion, the men stood up and formed into four groups which were led by armed soldiers, two in from, two behind, toward the lower part of the village. One of the first groups went into a barn belonging to my parents (the Laudy barn), about thirty yards from my observation post ».

The men were then divided into the seven barns as follows : Laudy, Milord, Désourteaux, Denis, Bouchoule and the Beaulieu garage and barn.

Interior of a tragic barn.

The killing of the men in the barns

The only male inhabitants who escaped the slaughter were in the huge Laudy shed. They are Messieurs Roby, Hébras, Borie, Darthout and Broussaudier.

First witness' testimony

We were able to meet and question M. Roby. M. Roby was born on the 15th January, 1926 at Basse-Forêt where he now lives with his parents. We now faithfully repeat his account :

« The group shut in the barn where I was included, amongst others, Brissaud, the village cartwright, Compain, the confectioner and Morliéras, the hairdresser. We had hardly arrived when the Germans made us get rid of the two carts which were in the way. Four soldiers then made us go to the inside of the building and levelled machine guns at us in crossfire to shop us escaping. They spoke amongst themselves and laughed whilst examining their weapons. Suddenly, five minutes after our entrance into the barns, as if in obedience to a signal like a powerful explosion, that I judged to come from the Market Square, they gave a loud cry and cowardly opened fire on us. The first to fall were protected from the strafing by the bodies that fell on them. I threw myself flat out, head between my arms but bullets were ricochetting off the wall near me. Dust and gravel made it hard for me to breathe. The injured were crying out, others for their wives and children !

« Suddenly the machine-gunning stopped. The torturers walked on top of our bodies to finish off at point blank range with their revolvers any injured person they saw still moving. I waited with terror for the bullet that was meant for me. I was hit in the left elbow. Around me the cries diminished and shots petered out. Finally, we were engulfed in silence, a heavy, anguished silence, broken nevertheless by a few stifled groans.

« The blood hounds then began to pile on us anything that would burn within their reach : straw, hay, faggots, cart slats, ladders and so on.

A corner of the market-place.

« Now not everybody around me was dead. A few low words were exchanged between those who were unhurt and those only injured. I turned my head slightly and recognized one of my friends covered in blood and still gasping. Would I end up the same way ? Some footsteps were heard : the Germans were back. They set fire to the pile of straw covering us. Flames spread quickly, filling the whole shed. I tried to flee but the weight of my friend'bodies hindered my movement. What was more, my injury stopped me moving my left arm. After a desperate effort I managed to release myself. I stood up, expecting to get a bullet but the torturers had left the barn.

« The air was becoming unbreathable. Then I noticed a hole in the wall that was, besides, some way off the ground. I succeeded in getting through it to find a hiding place in an adjoining storeroom. Four of my friends had made it before me : Broussaudier, Darthout, Hébras and Borie. I then slipped under a pile of beans and straw that was near me. Borie et Hébras hid behind some faggots ; Boussaudier curled up in a corner ; finally Darthout, struck with four bullets in the legs and bleeding everywhere asked for a little room to be made next to me. We held each other closely like two brothers and waited anxiously listening to every sound from outside. Alas, our ordeal was not over ! Suddenly, a German entered, stopped in front of the pile of straw sheltering us and set fire to it. I held my breath an we tried to avoid making the least movement but the flames were burning my feet. I was lying on top of Darthout who was motionless. I risked a glance up : the S.S. man had left. At the same moment Broussaudier was crossing the storehouse ; he had found a new exit. I followed him a few paces behind, pressed by flames, and arrived not far from a hutch that Broussaudier had entered and I followed in after. Without a moment's hesitation I dug a hole in the earth with my right hand and my foot then covered myself with any available debris. We stayed about three hours in this shelter. But suddenly the fire reached that in its turn and smoke got to our throats. I covered myself with my right hand to protect myself from embers falling from the roof and burning my hairy skin. A third

A charred body in a tragic barn.

time we had to flee the flames. I noticed a narrow passage between two walls and freed the entry to it ; so there we were crouched down and breathing a little fresh air. But we could not stay long in this place.

« We got up cautiously and made our way to the Market Square, well aware that there mustn't be any German soldier or guard. Broussaudier went out to spy. No one was there. Could we go... ? A last look left and right and we left as quickly as we could towards the cemetery. Thick scrub barred our way but nothing could stop us. We crossed through the bush and finally reached safety in the middle of a coppice. We hugged each other, such was our joy at being still in the land of the living. I had to spend the night in the middle of a rye field and reached my home at Basse-Forêt the day after, Sunday, at 11 o'clock ».

Statement of a second witness

The statements of the four escapees from the barn fully corroborate that of M. Roby.

M. Darthout, especially, confirms the emprisoning in the shed, the gunning and the massacre. He clarifies that the doors of the building were guarded by half a dozen soldiers armed with machine guns.

« I was hit in the first strafe », M. Darthout said, « by two bullets in the shins. I went down and then got two more in the thighs. My friends began falling on top of me. In a few seconds everyone was on the floor and I was covered in bodies. The machine gun kept firing. From the middle of a nightmarish din I could hear the groans and complaints of the injured. I remained crushed and flat out. My friend's blood was running over me. Every now and again I heard the sound of a breech being loaded then a shot... then nothing. My head was buried in dust and I was waiting for my final shot !

« The firing stopped and the heavy steps of the Jerries could be heard in the street. They came back into the shed, climbed into the corpses, talking and laughing. I was careful not to show any sign of

A charred trunk of a man, Laudy barn.

life. The assassins covered us with hay and faggots then left again. Then my hand brushed against another hand, I gripped it and it responded likewise.

« It was my friend Aliotti : « Both my legs are shattered. » He murmured. Then other low voices arose. Friends were still alive there. Duquerroy, the village guard lamented « My poor children, my legs are broken ! » Another, unhurt, put his head cautiously out : « The door is open ! » he reported. We could see the Germans moving in the road ; there was no escape. We could hear them talking : they had switched on a radio. It was a German speaker then came some music ! Next to me, Aliotti called for his wife and his children then bid us farewell !

« The Germans came brusquely into the barn and proceeded to set fire to the straw. Flames came up near me, burning my hair. I warded them off my hands and they were burned too. I turned round to crawl underneath the corpses away from the fire but at that moment I felt a terricble burn on my shoulder. The pain was so fierce I couldn't stand it. « Better die from a bullet in the skin than to be burnt alive ! » I thought. With difficulty I stood upright above the flames expecting the shot that would finish me off but the S.S. had gone and the door was shut. I fled from the flames to the far end off the barn. Soon there were five of us there, dismayed to watch all our friends being burned alive. Looking around to escape, we saw a hole in a barn wall that was in bad repair and one of us tried to make it larger. We got through to find ourselves in a hay store and hid ourselves in a hay store and hid ourselves in some straw. Then a German came in and set light to it with some matches. We had to leave our place of safety. Someone helped me to walk and we buried ourselves in a rabbit hutch.

« As I said, there were five of us in a group but one of our friends, M. Poutaraud, a mechanic, left on his own. He was spotted by the Germans just when looking for somewhere to flee to. His body was subsequently found stuck in a gate. We stayed in our bolt hole till about 7 p.m., then, still under cover of a smoke screen we made it to the Market. Square and after we had crossed that, I hid in a hedge about thirty

Body of M. Poutaraud the garage owner in the place where he was shot.

yards from the cemetery. I stayed there until nightfall when I could escape under cover of darkness ».

Two points of note arise from this testimony : firstly, from what we have learnt of the injuries of Messieurs Darthout, Aliottti and Two points of note arise from this testimony : firstly, from what we have learnt of the injuries of Messieurs Darthout, Aliottti and Duquerroy, who were hit in the lower limbs, the Germans fired low into their victims' legs ; secondly, men still living were set on fire. M. Darthout's statement establishes that they were still speaking ; those injured less were able to escape but those more seriously hurt were certainly burnt alive.

That, then, is the bare account of the horrific scene of carnage in the Laudy barn. We must presume that what happened in the five others in no way fell short of the cruelty and horror depicted in this barn.

We may here remark that a witness heard a direct echo of one of these frightful tragedies. Mme Lang reported :

« Suddenly, in the Milord shed, which was about six yards from the house where I was hiding, I heard the most heartrending screams and cries for help with intermittent strafes of gun fire ».

This statement is a useful inclusion, constituting the only evidence in our possession of events in barns other than the Laudy barn. For although five managed to escape there, unfortunately none escaped from the others, which must therefore keep their tragic secrets to themselves.

Findings in the tragic barns

Statements of the witnesses are corroborated by findings in the six barns the day after the massacres acted out in them.

All that remained of these buildings were the walls, capped with tuff and half collapsed. The floors were covered in rafters, some more, some less burnt, stones, tiles and various other materials. Numerous corpses and human debris were found there.

Charred body of Doctor Paul Désourteaux.

Bullet marks are still visible inside some of the sheds, scattered on walls opposite the entry doors.

The report, meticulously and expertly drawn up by M. Bapt, health inspector of Limoges, sets out the following details as to corpses in the various barns :

1. Barn of M. Bouchoule, baker, at the Market Square near the church : charred debris and bones of men, women and children ; also a corpse, head and trunk partly charred, to all appearances that of a man ;

2. Milord Barn : bone and charred debris ; 7 men's corpses found by the teams from Saint-Victurnien ;

3. Garage of M. Désourteaux : bones and charred debris ;

4. Warehouse of Mme Laudy, née Mosnier : bones and charred debris : 30 partly charred corpses, only of men, were brought up by teams from Saint-Victurnien and buried in the communal grave ;

5. Shed of M. Beaulieu : 20 to 25 corpses including that of M. Besson ;

6. Wine storehouse of M. Denis : bones and charred debris of men and women.

Denis garden mass grave. In the garden of the Denis barn a pit in which a certain number of corpses had been thrown was discovered. This pit was dug by the Germans to conceal traces of their crime. About 25 men's corpses were recovered including that of Doctor Désourteaux. A tobacco ration card in the name of M. Denis was also discovered.

This same report mentions the discovery along the road beside the cemetery to the left, level with the last house, of the corpse of M. Poutaraud, the mechanic ; This was taken away by his brother-in-law from Limoges.

The report of the mayor delegate of Oradour, M. Moreau :

« The bodies of victims discovered in the sheds and garages were completely disfigured by the fire, hence unrecognizable. Similarly, in the barns of Messieurs Laudy, Milord and Bouchoule no identification was possible ».

Concerning the other four barns, only the following identifications could be made :

Beaulieu Barn : Robert Pinède, Jean Valentin, Léonard Bardet, Louis Chapelot, Jean-Baptiste Nicolas, Pierre Moreau, Lucien Moreau, Jean-Baptiste Lavergne, Jean Lavergne, Léon Peyroulet, Jean Jackow and Albert Mirablon.

Denis Barn : Doctor Désourteaux, the mayor, Jean-Baptiste Tournier from Limoges and Jean Tessaud.

Désourteaux Barn : Jean Roumy.

Note that M. Bapt's report mentions the discovery of charred remains of women and children in the Bouchoule Barn and remains of women in the Denis wine storehouse. No doubt, these were poor victims, apprehended at the last moment and added at random to the men's group.

The massacre of women and children in the church

While the frightful killing of the men was being carried out, yet more savage and horrific was the massacre of the women that was taking place. It is beyond imagination and constitutes an indelible stain for the army that made it their responsibility.

There was only one escapee from this new carnage, Mme Marguerite Rouffanche, née Thurmeaux, who came from Limoges and was 47 years old. Her testimony represents all that can be known of the action. In the killing she lost her husband, her son, her two daughters and her grandson, aged seven months. She gave us this statement :

« At about 2 p.m. on the 10th June, 1944, after bursting into my home, German soldiers summoned me to go to the Market Square with my husband, my son and my two daughters.

« Already quite a number of inhabitants of Oradour had assembled there, yet still from every direction men and women, then chil-

Madame Rouffanche, sole witness to the massacre in the church.

Interior of the church.

dren coming separately from the schools, were flowing in. The Germans split us into two groups, one of women and children, another of men. The first group, which I was in, was led off by armed soldiers to the church. It included all the women of the town, especially the mothers, who went into the holy place carrying their babies in their arms or pushing them in little prams. There were also all the schoolchildren. I would estimate the number of people present there to be several hundred.

« Shoved together in the holy place, we became more and more worried as we awaited the end of the preparations being made for us. At about 4 p.m. some soldiers, about 20 years old placed a sort of bulky box in the nave, near the choir, from which some strings were led out and which they ran along the floor. These strings were lit and the flames passed to the apparatus which suddenly produced a strong explosion with dense, black, suffocating smoke billowing out. The women and children, half choked and screaming with fright, rushed towards the parts of the church where the air was still breathable. The door of the sacristy was then broken down by the pushing force of a very frightened group. My daughter was killed near me by a bullet fired from outside. I owe my life to the idea I had to shut my eyes and pretend to be dead.

« Firing burst out in the church then straw, faggots, and chairs were thrown pêle-mêle onto bodies lying on the stone slabs. I had escaped from the killing and was without injury so I made use of a smoke cloud to slip behind the altar. In this part of the church there are three windows. I made for the biggest window which was the one in the middle and with the help of a ladder which was used to light the candles, I tried to reach it. I don't know how but my strength was multiplied. I heaved myself up to it as best I could and threw myself out of the opening that was offered to me through the already shattered window. I jumped about nine feet down.

« When I looked up I saw I had been followed in my climb by a woman holding out her baby to me. She fell down next to me but the Germans, alerted by the cries of the baby, machine-gunned us.

The woman and the mite were killed and I too was injured as I made it to a neighbouring garden. I hid among some rows of peas and waited anxiously for someone to come to help me. That wasn't until the following day at about 5 p.m. ».

Since, as we have said, Mme Rouffanche was the only person to escape alive from the tragedy that unfolded in the church, we must keep strictly to her account. Any details over and above these would only amount to story-telling.

Findings in the church

Findings included in the various reports that we have to hand and those that we made ourselves in the holy place fully corroborate Mme Rouffanche's testimony even adding certain details as to this terrible massacre. The church was the scene of a violent fire. The roof was completely destroyed. The vault of the nave was treated mercifully by the fire and was still in place the day after the killing but has recently fallen down. The walls, blackened by the flames, are still up. The main altar was partly destroyed, the right chapel altar disappeared but the one in the left chapel was spared. The fire was less developed in that part than in the rest of the building. The four sculptures of important people, including the famous « chabre-taire », which happened to be in that part of the church, were untouched by the flames.

A report from the bishop's office states : « The main altar was shattered in certain areas by the bullets and hammers, the taberna-cle was smashed in front and behind and the communion table was torn out and twisted ». The bells melted under the intense heat and are now nothing but a shapeless mass of bronze spread over the stone slabs.

Mme Rouffanche stated that many shots were fired in the holy place. Indeed, the wall around the vestry window shows numerous bullet marks. The walls opposite the main entrance door also show several impact marks. The marble tablets on which were written the names of inhabitants of Oradour who died in the 1914-1918 war were shot through in some places and had hence come loose from the wall. This finding indicates that numerous shots were fired from the entrance door. Other volleys were also fired off from inside the holy place. Indeed a large number of cartridges were discovered. We found some there ourselves.

The Bishop's office's report was drawn up according to findings of seminarists who carried out the removal and burial of the corpses and states that hundreds of cartridges were found on the ground as far as the first third of the church.

This would indicate that the Germans penetrated fairly far inside the holy place to proceed with their tragic gunfire attack. In any case, bullet marks visible on some of the walls speak volumes in this matter.

Similarly, large blood spatters stain two of the left side chapel walls.

How many people met their death in this church ?

The report from the Bishop of Limoges's office indicates : « In two thirds or even just half of the building, built to seat 350 people, the number of women and children piled up there can be estimated at over 500 ».

The first people to enter the church found that the floor was covered with a thick layer of cinders and human debris, a nauseating magma of flesh and bone. Amid this layer lay a certain number of more or less charred and unrecognizable corpses.

M. Bapt, the health officer, in his report, relates :

« In the first day's examination, we discovered a considerable quantity of women's and children's bones in the church and the sacristy ». He goes on to state that bones and charred debris, including the foot of a child of about six, were found next to the main altar. In the right side chapel, where the fire was less intense, the wooden confessional box remained intact ». The report states that

Interior of the church. Altar and commemorative plaque of the dead of 1914-1918 shot through by Nazi bullets.

the corpses of two ten to twelve year old children were found in it and establishes that a large quantity of women's and children's debris and bones were collected from under the remains of collapsed floorboard in the sacristy.

The report continues : « There is a small side exit door situated in the right side chapel and the nave. The torture victims must have hoped at a certain time that it had been left open and that it would be possible for them to escape ! A large number of them moved over to that side. A pile of cinders, bones and charred flesh was indeed found there, and in much greater quantity than in the rest of the church. But, alas ! the door was firmly closed and the unfortunates could only defer the fatal moment a few seconds longer ».

M. Bapt's report estimates the amount of human remains at this place to be about a cartload. A police report says that the numerous pieces of jewellery, wedding rings and metallic objects discovered there lead one to surmise that hundreds met their death there. It states that stairs leading up to small exit door had disappeared under the cinders and bones.

A certain number of bodies were also discovered not far from the church. The health inspector's report mentioned above specifies that the corpses of eight children and two women were found in the lean-to under the presbytery. Recognizable amongst these were Mme Hyvernaud, Mademoiselle Marie-Rose Bastien and the children Raymond and Georges Thomas.

The report indicates besides that two isolated graves were discovered in the herb garden with the corpses of Mme Joyeux, née Hyvernaud and her child.

Lastly, it mentions a mass grave next to the small door of the church containing ten corpses and human debris representing fifteen people.

The mothers certainly brought their new born into the church. Several babies'remains were found there. Some mothers were holding them in their arms while others had brought them there in their

The confessional where the bodies of two children were found.

The oculus of the church bell-tower after the fire.

push chairs. We collected a number of these and have preserved them. Some were holed by several bullets and one had multiple perforations due to the explosion of a grenade.

Did the Germans fire at their victims' legs as they did in the barns ? All the evidence indicates that the torturers *aimed low* if only to get the poor children of Oradour. The babies' pram are undeniable proof of this. So if they aimed low, it is possible that the scene that unfolded at the Laudy barn could have been reproduced here, with women only injured in the legs collapsing one on top of another, and it is conceivable that some women who had been injured were able to remain motionless in order not to attract attention and thus escape further volleys of gun-fire. These would have been burned alive.

It is reasonable to think that among all these women and children, rushing, as we have just seen, in a crowd towards the right side chapel, some had their clothing alight and must have spread the fire from one to another. A large number of them were almost certainly burned alive. Their pitiful cries were heard in various parts of the town. The bishop's office report states that inhabitants two kilometres from Oradour could hear the clamour coming from the holy place.

Mme Lang gave the following account in this regard : « A terrifying sound erupted in the direction of the church which was just a few dozen yards from us. There was detonation after detonation followed by an immense clamour and terrified cries. Machine guns sounded off then a cloud of smoke rose up. Still so many clamours ! We stayed silent with fright, apalled and horrified. There was no doubt ! A terrifying massacre was being carried out just a few yards from us ».

The corpse of the woman who tried to escape the church after Mme Rouffanche was indeed discovered just in the place she indicated. Several testimonies and M. Bapt's report attest to the same. As regards the child's body, M. Aimé Fougeras, the present mayor of Oradour-sur-Glane, stated : « Accompanied by an escape, M. Martial Machefer, we proceeded to the garden where Mme Rouffanche had just been found. We had the idea to look in the presbytery closets situated in the alleyway. I found the body of a baby there ; the small corpse was lying at the bottom of the pit with its skull blown out. At the right temple was a large hole that looked as if it were caused by a blast of sub-machine gun fire at point blank range and out of the hole came brain matter. We placed it on the lawn of the garden and M. Moreau, mayor delegate of Oradour, collected it on Tuesday evening ». This child, eight months old, was identified by its unfortunate grandmother, Mme Ledot from Repaire.

We determined (and the evidence is still there) that the wall of one of these closets was covered with a large patch of blood. What scene could have taken place there ? Perhaps the child was knocked out by throwing his head against the wall. It is a plausible hypothesis and the one which is most believed in the region.

It is to be noted that on the 12th June, 1944, Father Vignéras, the

Pile of human ashes in the church.

curate of Javerdat, found a baby's nappy, still with safety pin in, next to the church and which still preserved the shape of the child's body that was wrapped in it. This could not be preserved.

ATROCITIES

While these terrible massacres were being executed in the barns and in the church, other S.S. detachments were unleashed in the village, committing the worst atrocities.

No one survived these little known scenes and the only witness were found but, as we shall see, their discovery throws nonetheless an awful light on horrific scenes unfolding at the time.

The torturers forced their way into the houses of the town and killed all the inhabitants who had escaped their first searches, especially those who, due to physical infirmity, were prevented from getting to the assembly point. One official report says « in this way, aid teams found bodies of some handicapped elderly people in various houses who had been burned in their own home ».

In the Rue Emile-Désourteaux, the charred remains of M. Giroux, a paralysed man of 75, were found still lying on the mattress of an iron bed. We ourselves determined the existence of charred bones. No bullet or even traces of any projectile in the vicinity were discovered despite meticulous searching carried out there, especially by ourselves.

One of that man's neighbours, M. Dupic senior, was found so carelessly buried in his garden that his hand was sticking out of the ground.

A special envoy of the French Interior Force who visited Oradour in the first few days specified that the charred remains of a father, mother and three children were gathered from inside a baker's oven. We ourselves found, not far from This baker's oven, a fire damper, still half full of coal, in which was discovered human bones (lumbar vertebrae) in an advanced state of charring. Faced with such a finding, it is clear that one is allowed to surmise a very great deal.

A pit must be mentioned that was found on the Lauze farm at Picat's home, containing numerous corpses. These were in such a state of decomposition that no identification was possible and we were obviously compelled to leave them as they were without attempting to move them. It cannot be ascertained whether these unfortunate victims perished in gunfire or had been buried alive, as some asserted. No cartridge was found in the area nor could any bullet traces be detected.

That is how those executioners went cynically about their job, throughout the village, machine gun and revolver in hand. No one was to survive that carnage, a man-hunt that was organised in irrepressible fashion. Anyone entering the town was stopped and shot down on the spot.

One escapee, M. Armand Senon, reported the following fact :

« Immediately after the assembly, I noticed a group of six or seven young people, not from the village, arriving by bicycle at the Market Square. They were surrounded by German soldiers and made to wait a few moments until an officer arrived from the lower town to meet them. He seemed to give orders to those surrounding them then they were made to leave their bicycles against a wall on the Market Square and were taken in front of M. Beaulieu's forge. There they were all shot with a machine gun ». A tragic end to a weekend's outing !

Mothers frightened by the shots that were crackling in the town ran from surrounding villages to try to bring home their children who were in class in the schools of Oradour. They were immediately stopped and without pity escorted to the death scene. We mention also Messieurs Duvernay and Raymond who were killed by machine gun fire in front of their children.

A shopkeeper, Mme Milord, was warned by friends, after returning from a journey, about what was happening in the village. They told

Prams of babies shot through by Nazi bullets and grenades.

her not to go all the way home, they tried to stop her but to no avail — her husband and children were in danger, so she ran to her terrible destiny !

M. Joyeux recounts the following episode :

« At the time, M. Foussat was with me at the village of Bordes. At about 7 p.m., seeing that the gunfire was petering out, he said to me : I am going back to the town ! My papers are in order. There's no danger. He went ahead a hundred yards waving a white handkerchief and climbed a small rise. But he was immediately machine-gunned down ».

Some inhabitants perished in a similar way but it is not possible to ascertain anything of the scene in which they played the victim's role. Near Bordes, the corpse of M. Villoutreix was found, with a large hole in his abdomen ; near the village of Masset, the corpse of M. Michel Avril, whose motor scooter was found in the Glane. M. Lachaud, shot by a dum-dum bullet in the head, was not immediately buried by the German camouflage teams. He was found with his skull blown out.

It has been said that the corpse of the parish priest was found in the church lying near the main altar. Another administrative report, however, stated that three priests were killed in the holy place. In fact no churchman's corpse was found there. On that day there were indeed three priests in the town : Father Jean-Baptiste Chapelle, 71, who had been at the parish for 33 years, Father Lorich, a priest from Lorraine and a young seminarist by the name of Emile François-Xavier Neumeyer. The first two were seen in the groups at the Market Square whilst the third disappeared without trace.

FINDINGS

In confirmation of the tragic facts we have just related, M. Bapt, the public health officer of Limoges'official report specifies that the following corpses were found ;

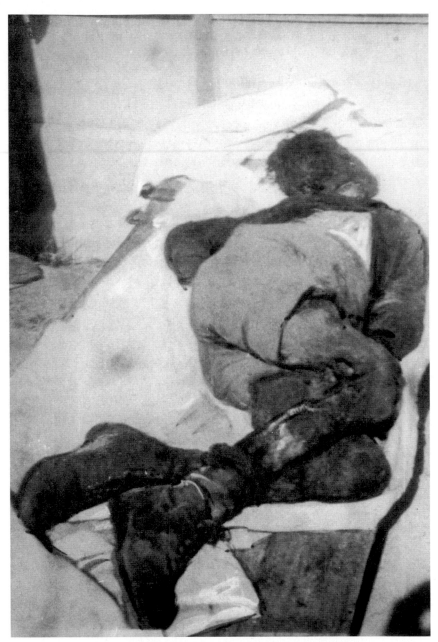

Trunk of a child taken up from a mass grave.

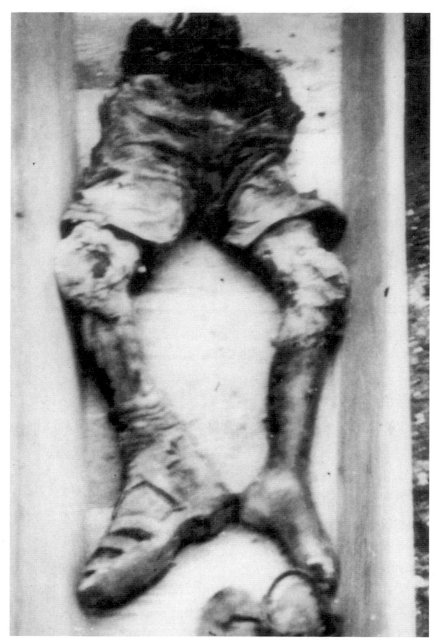

What is left of a poor child martyred in the church.

Pub of M. Mercier, Puygaillard

In the cellar, under a stone staircase, charred bones apparently of a woman and small baby.

La Brégère hamlet

A corpse found by M. Brun from Séguières on the afternoon on the 14th June. Being the body of Mme Victor Milord.

Bouchoule Bakers

Corpse of M. Milord, taken up by the Milord family of Dieulidou on Wednesday 14th in the afternoon. Being the corpse of M. Bouchoule (charred trunk and head). One corpse in the fire damper.

Farm of M. Picat

In the well, situated in the farmhouse courtyard, corpse of a woman and other human debris.

Garden of M. Dupic

Corpse of M. Dupic, taken up by M. Quériaud of Cieux on Thursday 15th June.

Town Hall garden

Corpse of a young man of twenty, unidentified.

Bordes Road

Pierre Raymond, taken up by his family. M. Foussat, miller, taken up by his parents. Michel Avril, taken up by M. Laroudie. Léonard Lachaud, taken up by his family. M. Duvernay, taken up by his family.

In a small house next to church

Charred remains of a woman recognized by her father M. Ledot. Being Mme Devoyon.

Further finding

We took not ourselves, and in the presence of M. Cordeau, the official guide to the ruins, of the remains of three bicycles left along a wall of the Market Square, wich belonged to the group of men chot in front of the Beaulieu barn. These have been preserved by us.

The escapees

Some people managed narrowly to escape the killing. A few young people, who, at their age, evidently had everything to fear from the Germans, hid themselves in their homes as soon as they arrived, then fled, most by crossing the garden fences situated behind their houses. Some were able to reach the countryside with ease.

As M. Paul Doutre, 21 years old, was a draft dodger, he did not want to go to the assembly point, but stayed at home. The S.S. tried to burn him alive in his own house.

Here is his statement :

« I was hiding behind my shutters and from the window could see my parents making their way towards the Market Square. I then hid in the workshop situated behind the house, but when it caught fire I attempted to get out of my hiding place and tried to save some special papers and keepsakes. Some German soldiers spotted me and forced me under threat of arms to go back to my hide-out. They then kept guard in front of the door to stop me fleeing.

« When I saw the flames starting up in the room where I was, I managed to fool the guards watching over me and escaped into the garden where I hid in a vegetable patch.

« Suddenly the roof caved in, and the Germans, thinking I was dead, left their position. While they were going, they passed close to me and I heard one of them say « Kaput ».

M. Darthout also notes : « A repatriated prisoner, M. Crémoux, recounted to me that when the Germans came into the town of Oradour, he was alerted and managed to reach the countryside, where he dived into a stream in order to hide himself. He remained under cover with only his head out of water, and saw two S.S. men going past. M. Crémoux, who understands German, heard one of them victoriously admit to the other : « I killed twenty six of them ! ».

M. Machefer, who lived, as did M. Armand Senon, in a house situated on the Market Square, was similarily forewarned in time of the danger which threatened : « When the Germans arrived in Oradour », he stated to us, « I was alerted in time to escape across the fields. My wife, who advised me to flee but herself failed to follow me, went to the assembly point. But alas ! I was never to see her again ».

To these escapees we would add the names of : M. Bélivier, aged 18, who hid in his orchard ; M. Brissaud a 17 years old cartwright, who saw that his garden was targeted and hid in his attic until it was clear to flee ; M. Hubert Désourteaux, son of the mayor of Oradour, who hid in a cubbyhole of his house. M. Aimé Renaud, Mme Jeannine Renaud, Mme Maria Robert, M. Armand Senon, whose tragic odysee has been recounted above and who fled for safety in his orchard where he remained hidden for 24 hours ; M. and Mme Lang and Mme Raynaud, who, thanks to their extraordinary coolness, managed to leave their house while it was in flames.

We must also mention : M. Litaud, former postman ; Mme Lauzanet, a woman in her sixties ; and finally two young Israeli girls by the name of Pinède, and their younger brother, who managed to escape the massacre by fleeing under the Germans' noses.

An entire family was able, miraculously, to avoid the tragic destiny of their compatriots : the husband, wife and children as well as a

The tragic oven of the Bouchoule bakery.

lady friend. They had resolved not to go to the Market Square and remained at home. When an S.S. man arrived to make a search of their house, he discovered the two women and the children and escorted them to the assembly point. The husband, who had hidden in a bedroom escaped the search, but another German surprised him in his hiding place and with great brutality made him come out. He found himself once again in the road with the two women, and the two children. The group was accompanied by one soldier, but whilst the guard was handed over to another, they managed to deftly slip away without their overseers noticing and reached the surrounding woods.

Some inhabitants' lives were saved because they were absent from Oradour during that afternoon. We cite, for example, two people who had decided to go fishing, artisans who worked in the area. Other were :

M. Desvignes, butcher, was at Saint-Victurnien market which took place exactly on that day ;

M. Daniel Senon, postman, was on his rounds ;

M. Pister, electrician, was on service at the Aurence depot ;

M. Deglane, cobbler, was out of town ;

M. Hébras Jean was working near Veyrac ;

M. Bardet, quarrier, was also working outside Oradour ;

M. Desroches was at Cieux ;

M. Garraud was hidden in a garden with M. Robert Besson ;

M. Descubes was with family near Javerdat ;

M. Hyvernaud was on his smallholding near Saint-Gence ;

Mme Montazeaud, wife of the notary, and her daughter, Mlle Compain, the baker's daughter, M. Eugène Leblanc, M. Emile Redon and M. Aimé Darthout had all gone to spend the day at Limoges. Some of these arrived at Oradour by the night tram.

On their return, they never again saw members of their families who had remained in the town.

The tram episode

Two trams from Limoges entered the town during the afternoon. The first to arrive was a test train and only tramway employees were in it. One, M. Chalard, got out but was brought down by a shot while he was walking across the bridge. The Germans got rid of his corpse by throwing it into the Glane where it was found. The tram was then sent back in the direction of Limoges.

The second train, this time carrying passengers, arrived at about 7 p.m. ; i.e. during the burning of the town.

Mlle Marie Gauthier, born on the 19th February, 1888, a grocer, living at 17, place de la Motte, Limoges, was one of the people in the tram and gave us the following account as soon as she arrived back at Oradour :

« This tram was stopped at the change over point of the Saint-Victurnien road by the Germans, who made us stay in the carriages. A soldier left by bicycle apparently to get orders and when he came back, he made all the passengers who were heading for Oradour get out. There were about 22 or 23 of us and we were heavily escorted to a point not far from the village of Les Bordes. We were made to cross the Glane on a narrow footbridge with the help of a tree trunk and then were directed to the Thomas house where the command post was situated.

« Our group was then stopped in the open country. The officer commanding the detachment held a discussion with the officer of the command post. The men and women were then separated and an identity check was made before we were brought back together again. After some hesitation and debate, suddenly the S.S. came forward, cocked their guns and made a circle around us. There was no doubt in our minds that they were preparing to execute us. Those were interminable moments of anguish and terror. Finally, after a somewhat heated discussion between the officer and the commander, they announced that we were free. We immediately hurried to reach the country ».

Child with skull smashed-in.

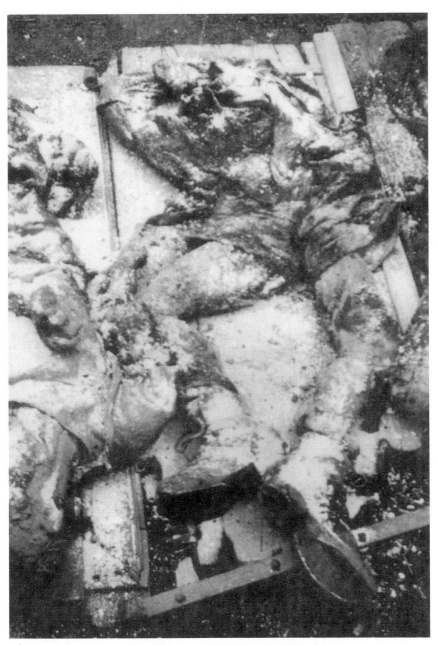

Bodies of women and children in the church.

Another passenger on the same tragic caravan confirmed to us that at that moment an interpreter shouted : « We are letting you go ! You can say that you were very lucky ! »

A young girl passenger was given a bicycle, evidently stolen, for her to get to her home more quickly. All the young girls of the village were massacred but they were gallant just the same ! During that time the order was given to send the tram back to Limoges where it arrived at around midnight.

Findings

The report of M. Bapt, the health inspector, confirms the discovery in the Glane, after the killings, of the corpse of M. Chalard, an employee of the Haute-Vienne tramway company.

Pillage and Arson

The S.S. ; at the same time as carrying out these killings, undertook a systematic pillage of the town. It is thought that this began during the time when the group of men were waiting at the Market Square. Each house was carefully searched and emptied of its contents. The village was rich and theft was bound to be lucrative : silver, linen, provisions, precious objects, everything was there. Lorries did not leave empty and safes were searched to the last inch.

M. Paul Brousse, honorary director of the Bank of France, who was designated as depository of the property recovered at Oradour-sur-Glane, reported to us the following finding :

« Bauche safe (in iron and concrete), found in Oradour at the home of M. Dupic, a fabric merchant. The safe had a key but could not be opened immediately because of the effects of the heat and we therefore had to take it apart. We were then able to establish that it was empty ».

The church had already been profaned but this did not prevent them from laying hands on the holy vessels in the tabernacle. Mon-

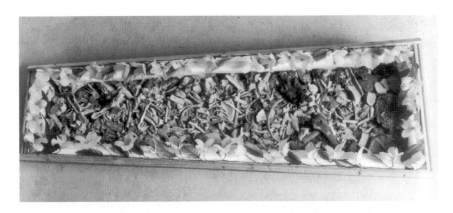

Various bones brought together during clearing-up operation in the church.

seigneur Rastouil, the bishop of Limoges, gave the following report :

« On Monday morning the S.S. returned to get rid of the masses corpses into large holes that were dug hurriedly. In the evening, canon Duron, senior priest of Saint-Junien, left for Oradour.

« I entered the church », he said, « to recover the holy contents. The tabernacle containing them had obviously been spared by the fire but that morning had been broken into and the ciborium taken away. I had no idea what could have happened to the hosts that were in it ».

As soon as Monseigneur Rastouil was told of this, he wrote a letter to General Gleiniger, commander of the Verbindungsstab of

Limoges, protesting about the matter in no uncertain terms. We print the following extract :

« You will understand my pain and indignation at learning that the church of Oradour-sur-Glane was defiled by the execution within its walls, of hundreds of women, young girls and children and profaned by the destruction of the tabernacle and removal of the consecrated ciborium...

« My office burdens me with the dupy to enquire as to the possibility of learning what has happened to the sacred bowls taken from the tabernacle of Oradour-sur-Glane and to recover them, not at all for their intrinsic value but rather on account of what they contained : the consecrated hosts ».

Not only did the Germans sack the town but even destroyed certain furniture with no valid reason or benefit to themselves. M. Martial Brissaud, 17, for example, gave the following testimony :

« I was at home at Oradour the day when the Germans arrived (on the 10th June, 1944). I wanted to flee, but the garden was watched so I hid in my attic. I could tell that before the house was set on fire, the S.S. smashed the furniture on the ground floor in a frenzy ».

Fire always follows the sack of a town. It is to be expected that the traces of pillage should be destroyed by fire and Oradour was no exception to this custom. The upper part of the town was the first to succumb to the flames :

To start the inferno, the Germans used grenades, tablet explosives and fire bombs. Houses, farms, shops and barns went up in flames and disappeared one after another.

The town was destroyed very quickly, the fire starting at 5 p.m., until at 10 p.m. the joyful town was no more than a mass of smoking ruins. A few neighbouring hamlets like « Les Brégères », and some isolated farms also suffered the same fate.

The night after the action

In the village was a house especially well furnished with food and which also, had a nice wine store. It was the house of M. Dupic Francois, the draper, and so contained a large amount of fabric. The S.S. spared it in the main fire and it was only the morning after that it was set alight.

This delay was due to their desire for more time to empty it as well as to provide a comfortable guard post in which spend the night. A group of German soldiers did in effect remain on the site until the following day and only left on Sunday at about 11 a.m. Was it not necessary indeed to destroy some excessively damning evidence of their crime ? After the war, responsibility must be allocated, consequently precautions had to be taken.

After the departure, then, of the bulk of the detachment, a certain number of S.S. men were busy in the midst of the rubble. It must be presumed that they were occupied with getting rid of corpses not completely burnt and burning what had resisted the fire. The escapee, Armand Senon, stated :

« During the night, I was hidden in a bush behind my house. All round me was the glowing of fires and I could still hear gunshots. At one moment, I saw a spot of light flickering near me ; it was a German at a guard post, seemingly making signals with an electric torch ».

He goes on to say : « On Sunday morning, the day after at early daybreak, I heard Germans in the town and saw the fire starting up again near the tram station. Afterwards, I realised that it was Dupic's house ».

Without doubt, during the night, the most atrocious orgies occurred in this house. M. Moreau, the mayor delegate, found in the ashes of this building the remains of twenty to twenty-five Champagne bottles !

They drank and binged in the Teutonic fashion, whilst other discoveries indicate clearly enough the monstrous nature of the scenes that these sadistic brutes gave themselves over to in the light of the fading glow of the fires.

Sunday, on the 11th June

M. Senon ended his story as follows :

« I was still hidden in the bush when daylight came and from the sound of lorries and motor vehicles, I got the impression that the Germans were leaving. I stayed for hours in my hiding-place hearing nothing but the crackle of stones and beams falling in the embers of the fire. During the afternoon I could hear patter of feet in the town and realised that the inhabitants of the area were returning. I then went in search of my parents and that was when I notices the corpse of M. Poutaraud stuck to a fence. He had been killed by a shot in the back and a horse was attached by a lead to his arm.

« I then waited, hiding behind a small shed until I decided to make my way to my father's house. I recognized M. Desvignes, the butcher, who told me that all the inhabitants of Oradour had been massacred by fire and that the whole village had been burned. All my family had disappeared ».

The fire in the Dupic house turned out to be ineffective in destroying traces of the abominable crimes that had been acted out there. Signs of theft there were no less evident than traces of the orgy. It was in fact in this house that the day after the crime, it was discovered that the safe that was emptied of its contents during the night.

The pillage of a town as rich as Oradour was evidently one of the most worthwhile. Upon reaching their billets, the Germans carried away items that they had pilfered and loaded them into the car of M. L..., which up to that moment they had avoided setting fire to. After hitching this car behind one of their lorries, they left in all haste in the direction of Nieul.

When they got to the village of La Plaine, the tow rope snapped, sending the car headlong into a telegraph pole and overturning it.

The help just after the drama.

The soldier at the wheel was seriously injured and was laid out in the lorry. While this was being done, other S.S. men hurried to the damaged car and pulled out obviously the fruit of their theft and transferred them into their own vehicle. When they had done that, they set fire to the car which was lying in the ditch and set off again.

This incident was related to us by M. Désourteaux, an eye-witness.

Monday, on the 12th June

Some Germans returned to Oradour on Monday morning at first light. They set to work at digging two pits in which they buried the more compromising remains of their victims. The larger of these was more than three metres long and was discovered, as we have already said, in the garden of the presbytery, close to the small door in the right side chapel. Amongst the half burnt human remains and debris of flesh and bones, a certain number of bodies, damaged beyond recognition by the effect of the fire, were collected.

As we have already mentioned, a second pit was dug in the small garden next to the Denis garage. This was at the corner of the main street of the town and the minor rue Dieu-lidou and was one of the six buildings in which the men of Oradour were shut and massacred. In this burial hole the bones and more or less charred human remains corresponding to thirty or so corpses were found. Only one was capable of identification, that of M. Désourteaux senior, president of the special delegation. He had been killed by two bullets in the chest and his wallet had also been pierced by them, which would seem to indicate that he did not suffer the same fate as the victims tortured in this shed. He was brought down separately, perhaps as a result of his protest against the monstrous deeds of his executioners. At the same time, a certain number of corpses had been buried by them in the fields in the neighbourhood of the town.

As they withdrew, the soldiers that constituted the rear guard detachment strafed the lower part of the town with machine gun fire

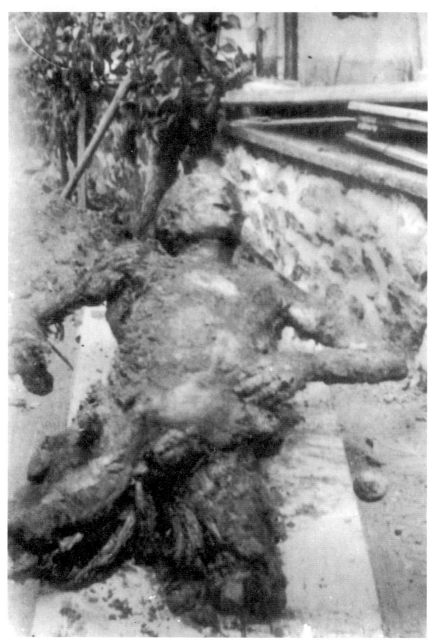

Charred body.

and left on the Limoges road, which would also lead them to Nieul. It is believed, indeed, that they came from one of these two towns and had been sent to Oradour to clean up any overly embarassing traces of this abominable crime as well as any piece of evidence that might associate them with it.

It is certain, however, that that morning, they burst into the private house of M. Puygrenier who had been away since the previous evening. When he tried to come home at about 7 a.m. he heard the sound of boots and voices coming from his house. He could hear German being spoken and wisely withdrew. When he came back to his house during the day, he found that his brandy had been drunk and that his eau de Cologne had been used ; lastly, a sum of money had been pilfered.

German officers, sent some days after to Oradour by the Kommandantur to carry out an « Enquiry » demonstrated the utmost moral qualities commensurate with their mission by swiping all the poultry left by the unfortunate inhabitants.

A sight of tragedy

At about 2:30 on Sunday afternoon, after the departure of the Germans, the first of the first aid teams arrived. Alas ! Death was victorious everywhere and no one was left alive in the village.

Walls, lashed by flames, stood out as far as the eye could see and everywhere, traces of incendiary bombs could be seen around windows.

In a moving article of the first edition of the *Centre libre*, M. Marc Bernard told that a large number of shop signboards in the little town had not been affected by the flames. We could, for example, pick out « Hôtel Milord », « Hôtel Beaubreuil », « Restaurant Dagoury », « Café du Chêne », and in simpler style « Baker's » and « Hairdresser ». Nothing in this death asylum was more insistent than these last vestiges of the boisterous, welcoming and jolly life of this local centre. The contrast between yesterday and today was so poignant

The bodies of the victims were placed on shutters to help in transport.

and overwhelming and a heavy atmosphere weighed on the shoulders of all those who were there to help.

Every roof, window and door had been prey to the flames, and two burnt-out little saloon cars, one of which belonged to doctor Désourteaux, were waiting hopelessly at the Market Square for their drivers, who alas ! would never return.

Animals, in search of shed or stable, wandered sinisterly into the deserted village.

After the tragedy of Oradour, most of the cats of the town took shelter in the house of M. Georges which had been spared from the fire because it was situated outside the locality. It was a moving spectacle to see all these Toms gathering at certain times in the courtyard of that welcome house looking for their food.

M. Bapt, the health inspector, was one of the first people to go into Oradour after the tragedy. This is how he so vividly depicted the sight of the martyred town at that time.

« Apocalyptic. Where once lay a dainty and charming little town with its peaceful and hard-working people, faithful to the old traditions of the Limousin, there existed nothing more than a mass of ruins and cinders. On the charred outcrops of walls, the signboard of a restaurant or grocer's could still be read, heaps of all kinds of material lay about everywhere, blocking the roads here and there ; bricks, ironwork, glass and so on ; supporting beams of old 15th century houses were still burning or lay about bitten by the fire ; worried swallows darted back and forth across the roads and squares amidst the ruins, searching for nests that would never more be found ; faithful yet fearful dogs lay down in the ashes of their houses, left slowly at our arrival, their tails drooping dejectedly and obstinately came back to their place as soon as we were further off ; farmhouse animals, such as rabbits, chickens and ducks who had escaped from their hutches or their roofs, taken aback by such unknown freedom, ran about in the peaceful gardens where a harvest of flowers was blossoming in the sunshine ; cows and bulls were

A body retrieved from a mass grave and placed on a shutter to be transported.

found lying in their usual place in their destroyed stables, amongst the ashes ; and standing amongst all these ruins was the old church with its square tower flanked by bartizans and the roof caved in, flame-licked walls covered by wide lashings of soot, the statues and mutilated altars and the floors strewn with cinders and on which a shapeless mass of bronze, all that is left of the bells that were melted by the fire, lying next to religious objects and bullet marks on the wall.

« And this is all that is left of Oradour, or rather not so, since there still remain within these ruins, the corpses, yes a crowd of corpses of men, women and children, an entire population, 700 or 800 or even more ».

Inside the houses all that remained were metal objects, but in what a state ! Scattered everywhere, could be seen buckled and shattered household items and bicycles twisted by the effect of the heat. In the barns, half burnt bodies of the victims were still distinguishable lying among the cinders. They appeared like tragic bronze statues to the astonished onlookers.

Faced with so much devastation and chagrin, confusion reigned in the mind and no one could hold back their tears. A few groups went over to the church, but all that could be found were tragic, bitter ruins. The roof had completely disappeared and the clock tower lifted up two long, bare and desolate arms to the sky in an expression of despair as if to make its last, anguished prayer. Monseigneur Rastouil, bishop of Limoges, gave the following moving account :

« Surprises... and lessons. On the outside wall of the church, the mission crucifix, recently plated over with aluminium, is intact and 50 yards away from the church, in the facade of a burnt house, is a second cross of wood, handing on the burnt wall, still upright and attached. It is He, always He, Christ stretching out His arms over the ruins.

« So we went into the church. Broken statues lay on the ground, but there was another surprising lesson : Over the left altar, two sta-

Ruins of the destroyed village (aerial view).

tues remain completely intact, that of Our Lady of Lourdes and, three or four yards away, that of Bernadette facing towards Marie and in prayer ».

Another witness stated :

« It was a ghostly sight inside the shaken, tormented and upset church. An acrid smell of burnt flesh rose up from the embers to grip your throat, and from the cinders, human remains cried out the lamentable end of those unfortunate victims. Here and there, small pitiful children's hands lay scattered and forlorn on the stone slabs and the feet of poor kids which had not been entirely burnt could be seen. In the confessional box the heart-rending corpses of two tiny children holding each other round the neck could be seen. They had been spared by the fire but bore the marks of bullet wounds from a revolver in the nape of the neck. Not far from there, the body of a young school teacher lay amidst the miserable remains of her pupils.

« One man suddenly recognized his wife. She lay in a terror-stricken pose, tightly holding one of her female relatives. He approached to separate them but his hand had hardly brushed their shoulders when to his great horror the two corpses suddenly crumbled away and disappeared into dust. All the time, the most distressing identifications were being made. One inhabitant of a neighbouring village whose nine year-old child had not returned from school the day before, found his little corpse frightfully disfigured ».

Pitiable Wrecks

Numerous objects carried by the unfortunate victims of the action or brought with them at the time of their death, were recovered from the ruins of the martyred city, especially from the church and the barns. Some of these were very impressive and we have conserved them to one day exhibit them in the church or in the display cases of *the Remembrance Building* which we envisage establishing in Oradour. Future generations must be given a concrete and irrefutable testimony of German barbarism. There are certainly as many such items as are necessary to bring a conviction before the court of History.

First, let us mention certain children's push chairs which mothers used to transport their babies to the place where they were tortured and, as we have said, many German bullet marks can be seen on them. One of them — and we cannot forbear the reminder of it — was completely ripped up by the explosion of a grenade.

A great quantity of jewellery was found in the church as well as in the barns comprising a large number of engagement and wedding rings, the majority made of gold, as well as numerous watches made of non-valuable metal such as steel or nickel. A certain number of handbag and wallet clasps were recovered also. The inventory which we have made of these sad relics includes a large quantity of coins, including a high proportion made of silver.

Otherwise, there were keys, many keys, lighters, some wallets containing personal papers and even bank notes which were more or less charred. One of these wallets, as we have already mentioned, was pierced by a bullet. A cigarette case and a spectacle-case were also shot through by projectiles.

We are in possession of numerous knives of all shapes and sizes. Remarkably, four of these, whose blades were especially long and pointed and which could therefore be used as weapons, were found out of their normal sheaths ; it would appear that some of the unfortunate men shut up in the barns thought to defend themselves when they saw that they were about to massacred.

An unbelievable number of corset stays, belt buckles and remains of metallic toilet objects, make-up bags, powder puffs and lipstick dispensers were found in the church, moving reminders of the last attempts to look pretty.

We have brought together numerous toys which belonged to the poor children of Oradour to reverently exhibit them in a special show case. There is no doubt that if there is one memory which will forever be engraved upon the soul of the children who are called to reflect upon this, it is that of the pitiful remains of the toys of their young friends who were so ferociously exterminated by the German ogres.

To conclude that section, we shall relate certain poignant discoveries which were also made in the holy place. Firstly, there was a stamped envelope which had not yet been posted and which was smeared with blood. It was addressed to the parish priest of Javerdat and contains a letter intended to be read by him. It was dated on the 10th June, 1944, the day of the tragedy at Oradour and in it the following sentence can be read : « I feel fine now. For me the sun shines here now ». The woman who wrote this sentence was to die the death of a martyr that the same day. She was carrying the letter, intending to post it. The blood stains visible on the envelope, were, it seems, from her own body. The letter was subsequently sent to the addressee.

We also draw attention to a song carefully copied onto a page of letter paper in a handwriting which appears to be that of a young girl. The following extract is a faithful transcription of one of the verses :

Hear the chimes of happiness
Resounding boldly in my heart.
Far from the weight of weariness,
How the ding dong song of sweetness
Peals in the bell tower of my heart !

How dramatic and upsetting was the destiny of this unfortunate child who brought such an intoxicating call to life and happiness into the place where she was martyred.

Finally, the Rév. Vignéras, priest of Javerdat drew our attention to the page of a school exercise book belonging to young Marguerite Simon, 11 years old, and on which in her best handwriting she had written : « I resolve never to hurt people ». This child's decision, who fell victim to such savage deeds, deserves to be printed and publicised throughout Germany : A beautiful lesson given by

General view of the ruins.

Crossing of the Saint Junien and Javerdat road.

one insignificant of our children, to the proud, ardent zealots of the German Kultur !

Also among these miserable relics, buried in piles of cinders and human debris, were a considerable number of German bullets and cartridges.

German bullets

Although no firearms were found in the ruins, quantities of 9 mm. Revolver cartridges, bearing the inscription WRA 9 mm on their sleeves, as was also the case of some rifle cartridges.

M. Romério, a Public Works contractor, who was given responsibility for consolidating the ruins of the church, discovered six rifles cartridges of 50 mm in lengh near the main altar under piles of embers amidst human bones and other objects, bearing the following inscriptions on their sleeves :

— first cartridge : hrn St 39-43
— second cartridge : hrn St 40-43
— third cartridge : hrn St 41-43

The inscriptions on the sleeves of the three other cartridges were illegible on account of damage by fire and oxidation. We ourselves discovered a revolver cartridge bearing the inscription aso Stf 8-44 as well as several other rifle cartridges bearing the same letters and numbers. One of them however bore the inscription Kam St 42-5.

The assassins after the crime

The S.S. did not return to Saint-Junien after accomplishing their crime. One section billeted in Nieul, where our investigation uncovered particularly remarkable episodes. First of all, we must make known an event which depicts the mentality of the criminals of Oradour better than long phrases.

Numerous inhabitants of the surrounding area testify that on the evening of the tragedy, S.S. men fired volleys from automatic weapons along the road from the top of the lorries which were driving them to their billets, M. Henri Demange from Barre de Veyrac made the following declaration :

« On the 10th June, at about 8 p.m., I saw a German lorry loaded with materiel coming from Oradour in the direction of Nieul on which I saw and heard S.S. men singing and playing the accordeon ». Several other witnesses also confirm this testimony.

All the inhabitants confirm that the Germans were in an unusually excitable state upon their arrival in Nieul. They spread out into the streets, ejaculating loud cries. They declared themselves surprised by the quietness and correction of the welcome of the local people who did not yet know anything of what had happened in Oradour. They were suspicious. The officers decided not to remain alone but to sleep in the same room.

They had come back from a hard « expedition » and were very hot ! So they drank and drank and spent part of the night washing in the school toilets. There were stains difficult to remove !

Food and wine were wasted, it was time for a good blow-out ! They drank and ate, shouted, threatening death and fire. Some young women were forced to flee. M. Bouty, headmaster of the school at Nieul, gave us the following declaration in This regard :

« The S.S. arrived at Nieul on Saturday, 10th June, 1944 at about 10 p.m. with a half track at the head of the lorries. As soon as they had stopped on the square in front of the school, the German soldiers got out from their vehicles and a short while after, a small group of three or four men went towards the school. One of them violently kicked at the closed door where I lived. I opened it straight away and a soldier who spoke a little French, asked me : « School for 150 gentlemen ? » I showed them the classrooms which had been requisitioned the day before by a detachment of German soldiers at the same time as the two bedrooms of my personal flat and numerous rooms in the town. The soldiers settled in the classrooms and the whole night long, numerous lorries wheeled about in the school playground. The officers who were to take the rooms in my apartment did not return, and I learned later than they had mattresses brought into the room of a council building where they spent the night.

« On the following day, a Sunday, the German soldiers had meals prepared for them in the houses of the town of Nieul from the poultry which they had brought live in sacks. After their departure, I found a pot of home made jam and bottle of spirit, neither completely empty, on the lawn in front of my house and within the school court yard there were a dozen dead chickens, some of which had been plucked and decapitated ».

M. Paul Michot, a fitter at the Nieul broadcasting station and son-in-law of M. Laroudie, the butcher, gave the following details :

« In my father-in-law's house the Germans opened bottles of old wine which they had brought with them and which were found empty after they had left. They also had a number of ham shoulders. In the kitchen they roasted coffee beans. They also had lots of pigeons and rabbits ».

Asked if he noticed any suspicious objects which the Germans had brought with them, he replied : « I saw German soldiers in some lorries, wrapped in blankets nothing to do with the military. On Sunday, I also saw soldiers playing with two new bicycles in the school playground which they broke amidst laughter and vulgarity. On Monday the 12th, after these troops had left, I recovered the frames of the two bicycles, one of which had an identity plate in the name of Barthélémy, Oradour-sur-Glane. Besides this, a motor scooter belonging to M. Leblanc from Oradour-sur-Glane, was found in the park pond ».

During the billetting at Nieul, the eagerly expected scene unfolded : In two of the houses and perhaps in others, but certainly in two of them, money was shared out. Could this have been the splitting of the booty from Oradour ? Nobody in the village doubts this.

M. Michot stated : « An S.S. man who was lodging in my parents-in-law's house distributed banknotes, which he took from two huge boxes among his companions, through the dining room window. The Germans went around the town with their hands and pockets full of these pieces of paper ».

We asked Mme Riffaud, a restaurateur at Nieul, what had been the German's attitude in the locality. She answered : « Some Germans stayed with me bringing with them a live duck tied up in a bag. They asked me to put it on one side so as to take it away with them when they left Nieul. As I suggested that the animal was very likely to suffocate in the sack, one of them answered that if he gave out, then my husband and I would be kaput the day after. I replied : « After we have served you all day, you would surely not do that ! ». They replied :

« Oh ! Madam, we have done worse ! A bullet only makes the tiniest little hole ! » While saying these words, he aimed at me with his revolver. When I refused to show them the rooms of the house-maids who were employed in the establishment, these same Germans threatened to shoot me and my husband and to set the house on fire. I would add that along the Bellac Road, they killed a young 15 year old man, M. Doumeix, from Fougerat, who had tried to flee when he saw them ».

M. Bouty also revealed : « During the whole of the Sunday, German soldiers remained posted in the lorries. It was clear that the SS did not have a quiet conscience and realised very well the seriousness of the crime that they had accomplished, fearing reprisals from the exasperated population, who they thought might perhaps revolt ».

M. Bouty continued : « From time to time one of these vehicles would leave in the direction of neighbouring areas and I learnt that during one of these expeditions, a detachment had set fire to the Château of Morcheval, which is next to Nieul ».

Carcasses of burnt-out cars in a garage.

THE VICTIMS

The number of deaths at Oradour cannot be precisely evaluated. Given that the population was completely wiped out, it is impossible, at least for the moment, to carry out the enquiries that such an evaluation would necessitate. Neither should we forget that there were many refugees in the town and that on that very day many people foreign to the locality were passing through. Entire families have disappeared, in one, 24 victims. M. and Mme Deschamps were the unfortunate parents to lose their four young daughters.

M. Moreau, acting Mayor delegate of Oradour, has been able to account for the names of 636 victims so far. But it is generally considered that the number of persons massacred is not far from a thousand.

At the end of this work, we have published a list of persons whose bodies were identified and for whom a death certificate was issued. Accompanying that is a list of persons known to be in Oradour during the massacre and who have been simply declared as officialy missing.

BUILDINGS DESTROYED

As far as concerns the buildings in the town, figures drawn up by the mayor delegate show the following division of buildings which were destroyed :

Private dwelling houses	123
Work shops	26
Private and other garages	19
Storehouses	35
Barns	40
Sheds	58
Shops	22
Schools	4
Station	1

A total of 328 buildings destroyed.

EXHUMATION AND BURIAL

Responsibility for this was in the hands of Doctor Bapt, health inspector. We have already quoted a number of passages from his report and shall now proceed to give the essential sections :

« In accordance with instructions given to me and with the authorisation of the German authorities (Ausweis n° 11 of the Major General dated on the 14th June, 1944), I went with my partner, Doctor Bénech, to Oradour-sur-Glane to proceed with the interment of the victims and the burial of animal corpses and in order to take any sanitary measures.

« The commander of Praingy, under General Sigaud, regional director of passive defence, willingly gave me his assistance. The French Red Cross, the National Aid, the technical services and young people from the National Youth Aid Teams placed specialised teams at our disposal thus allowing us to accomplish rapidly the task that was entrusted to us and in the best conditions possible.

« The commander of Praingy, Doctor Bénech and I went to Oradour-sur-Glane on the afternoon on the 14th June along with twenty or so helpers from the Red Cross Emergency Teams.

« ...On the first day, four corpses were found. One in front of the Bouchoule bakery was of a man with only a charred head and trunk remaining whilst the arms and legs had been completely burnt. The second was found in the barn of Mme Laudy, trunk and head charred and arms and legs burnt away ; This was a woman's corpse recognized by one of her parents as that of Mme Desbordes. Lastly, in the garden belonging to Mme Laudy, not far from the barn we have just mentioned, there were found the corpses of a woman and a man, killed by bullets, slightly charred and easily recognizable. The woman, identified by M. H. Désourteaux, was a refugee from Lorraine ; the man was M. Thomas, a baker. These corpses were placed in coffins and buried in the cemetery.

« ... On Thursday the 15th, a tram from the Haute-Vienne Tramway Company brought us to Oradour along with the teams of the different services, there were in all 149 mens

« … Our operations continued in the following days : Friday 16th, Saturday 17th and Monday 19th in the following conditions :

« I. *Public order services* — Under the direction of the commander of Praingy, the public order service was carried out by one of the emergency teams available to us. Barriers were put up at the entrance of the town.

« II. *Clearing-up* — Technical services teams were given the task of clearing up under the authority of the commander of Praingy. Only the following buildings were cleared : Barns, garages and houses where corpses were presumed to be lying under the ashes.

« III. *Search* — From the very first day, teams of young people under the authority of the commander of Praingy were designated to search for Human or animal corpses, tombs and burial holes.

« IV. *Recovery of precious objects and papers* — Any objects that were found either on the corpses or in the ashes, purses, gold coins, jewellery, bonds and identity papers were either deposited at the Bank of France, in the rue Fritz-James establishment, or to M. Moreau.

« V. *Sites where human corpses were discovered* — On Tuesday the 13th June and on the morning on the 14th, a team comprising local people and volunteers from Saint-Victurnien had come to take away the corpses : precisely 35 were removed from the ashes by their efforts. Further, other victims were taken up and carried away on the same day by the inhabitants of neighbouring villages. As we have already indicated above where these corpses were found, we shall not return to the subject.

« VI. *Identification and burial of the victims* — The bodies of the identified victims were put into coffins and placed either in tombs or in special graves. On each of the graves a cross was placed with the name of the victim inscribed upon it. Bones and human remains as well as unidentified bodies were placed in two communal graves.

(This report was followed by a list of 28 persons identified at the time when it was drawn up. The number of victims that have now

A view of rue Emile Désourteaux.

been identified is 53 and we publish their names at the end of this work).

« VII. *Animal corpses* — Amongst the animals killed some died of asphyxiation and others were in part burnt.

In « Les Brégères » farm 8 carcasses, including 5 bulls or cows were found ;

« In the stable of Mme Laudy (tenanted by M. Senon), five partly burnt bulls were found ;

« In the farm of Mme Laudy (tenanted by M. Desbordes), were found three bulls and two asphyxiated heifers in a stable as well as the corpses of about thirty sheep in a sheep pen.

« All these corpses were burnt and their remains placed in three pits.

« VIII. *Health and disease prevention* — (Here follows the description of disinfection measures taken. We shall limit this account the section relating to individual protection).

« The team members whose job it was to take up the corpses and collect the human remains together were provided with rubber gloves. Besides this, those who carried out the exhumations, transport and interment of corpses were provided with masks saturated with eucalyptus essence against the nauseating smell which had been made all the worse on account of the extreme heat.

« *Incidents* — On Monday the 19th, when I had cycled over to the village of Les Bordes, a few frightened villagers came to warn us that German soldiers were in Oradour. Fearing some incidents, and to protect the men of my teams, I returned immediately.

« At the entrance of the town, I found myself faced with three German lorries, the first one armed with an unlimbered machine gun. Two sentries were watching the road and a dozen soldiers armed with sub-machine-guns were surrounding the abattoir whilst some others dismounted the wheels and tyres of one of the only two cars that had escaped the fire.

« I showed my Ausweis and when my identity was checked, I

The workshop of the wheelwright.

went into the town. I there learnt from M. Fichaud, that the German soldiers had loaded their vehicles with several bicycles belonging to our men. After some explanations he was able to get them back, but in the town the teams had stopped working and had dispersed into the countryside. They came to meet me again et the cemetery and it was at that moment that 15 or so shots were heard. The Germans had been firing on farmyard animals that had escaped into the fields.

The report adds, « I wish to thank all those who gave us their assistance, in particular the team of seminarists who were always willing to carry out the most painful, dare I say repellant, tasks ».

Incidents concerning the funeral service at Limoges cathedral

A Requiem Mass for the repose of the souls of the victims of Oradour had been announced by Monseigneur Rastouil, bishop of Limoges, for Wednesday 21st June at 9:30 a.m. at the cathedral.

Monseigneur Rastouil, in an account made by him of incidents given rise to by this ceremony, revealed that from Saturday to Wednesday, the German police did everything in their power to prevent its taking place. He confirms that, to this end, they spread a false rumour in the town that he had been arrested and that there was a mysterious bomb deposit underneath the cathedral. He states that an explosives dump was even simulated there. During the night on the 20th to 21st June, the muffled sounds of picks and hammers were heard, appearing to come from the crypt of the holy place. In fact, it was a team of workers working in the cellars of neighbouring houses.

« On Wednesday at 8:30 a.m. », the bishop of Limoges said, « the archpriest alerted me of the night work. The police were advised immediately and explored both cellars and basements.

« At 9:25 a.m. I went to the cathedral, where there was a dense crowd trying to get into an already filled church. The mass started and proceeded normally. At the last prayers, when I just about to put on the cope to give the absolution, the regional prefect warned me that the police did not feel at ease, that there was still some risk of danger and that I was requested if possible to cut short the ceremony.

« I felt very strongly my responsibility before a crowd so compact that all the side chapels were filled as on the great days of the display of the monstrance and which was also overflowing outside the building. Imagining in one second the frenzy which an explosion or collapse would provoke, I replied : « Tell the prefect that I will omit the absolution ».

« However I straightaway thought of the crowd who had seen the unusual movements of the police, the communications between the prefect and the bishop, and how they might be taken by surprise at the omission of the traditional absolution in such a ceremony. The crowd might have then gone wild seeing what they thought was a sudden departure on my part. The least panic might have brought about the deaths of several hundred people.

« So I turned to the packed crowd, numberless and dignified : « My brothers, for the dead of Oradour-sur-Glane, let us say the De Profundis ». After the psalm I continued : « Let us say Our Father and Hail Mary for the families of the victims ». I then left slowly, having greeted the regional prefect. No mines had been laid, but rather a trick, a shame to sabotage the funeral service in memory of the victims of Oradour-sur-Glane ».

As can be seen, it was even forbidden to pray for the unfortunate martyrs !

THE ASSASSINS

**Important documents revealed enabling
the discovery of the true reasons
for the massacre of Oradour,
the identification of the unit in question
and the names of some of the assassins**

On the 26th October, 1944, the press announced the capture of Lieutenant General von Brodowski and his second in command, Major Schradel, who were in command of the unit responsible for Oradour. Both were on their way to northern France, along with a few men on the troop, trying to reach Germany on foot. Major Schradel was arrested first in the Château of Grenant in the department of Haute-Saône on the 21st September. He had just shot three young people from the region as well as three nurses. He revealed that his chief had taken the direction of Corre. He was indeed discovered in a barn in that area.

The officers interrogating von Brodowski found a route note book on him and on its pages were written the following entries :

« *On the 11th June, 1944* — During an action of the troop on the 10th, the locality of Oradour (31 km south-west of Limoges) was reduced to dust and ashes.

« *On the 14th June, 1944* — A telephone call from Oradour advised me that 600 people had been killed. The entire male population of Oradour was shot... The women and children fled into the church which then caught fire as explosives had been hidden there. All the women and all the children died ».

This document was nothing but a web of flagrant inaccuracies : women and children fleeing for safety in the church, munitions sto-

Bodies placed in a barrow which will take them to the communal graves.

red there and an accidental explosion are as much lies as our readers can judge for themselves. Neither the testimonies received nor the findings made in the church reveal the existence of such facts.

But the nazis were not short of a story or two. They excelled even themselves concerning the reasons they invented to justify their crime on the 10th June. As a pretext, they asserted the existence of an armed attack against German soldiers and officers. According to some, this happened in the vicinity of Oradour whilst according to others in the town itself.

It is known that one S.S. man, a short while after his arrest, had asserted that on the 10th June, some kilometres away from the martyred town, the detachment he belonged to had been violently attacked by the maquis. The officer commanding the unit had then taken revenge on the first village he came to and which was Oradour-sur-Glane.

It is clear that the soldier had every reason to attempt to justify the crime of which he stood accused in this way. But the detailed enquiry which we carried out in the region was in formal contradiction with such allegations. In reality no attack happened in Oradour nor in the surrounding districts, no more on the 10th June than on any other day. We repeat that the Nazis had no valid reason to attack this peaceful town.

Besides this, there were no Maquis at Oradour-sur-Glane, and if the S.S. had decided on « this expedition » it was not because there were elements of resistance there, but rather because they knew very pertinently that there were not and that they could consequently commit their odious crime with impunity.

We repeat that there were neither munitions nor arms dumps of any sort at Oradour ; all the statements of the escapees are unanimous and formal in this regard. As we have said, Oradour was a calm and peaceful village. No German officer or soldier or any collaborator had ever been assassinated there. There were other reasons for the massacre of this population and we shall examine these

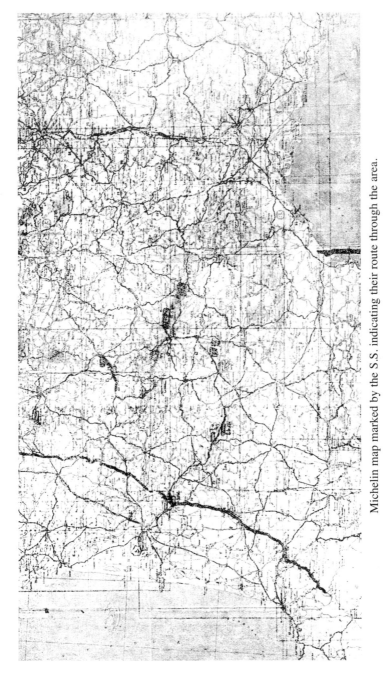

Michelin map marked by the S.S. indicating their route through the area.

in the sections which follow. Firstly however, where did the assassins come from and who were they ?

DISCOVERY OF A MAP
annotated by the perpetrators of the massacre at Oradour from which the itinerary followed by them since their arrival in France can be reconstructed

The assassins of Oradour left a number of documents on the scene of the crime which were collected after their departure. Monsieur Jean Villoutreix, living at Berthe in the township of Saint-Auvent, made the following statement :

« I certify having discovered, on the 16th June, 1944, in the field of Monsieur Bélivier from Les Brégères in Oradour-sur-Glane, a satchel which belonged to a German soldier who must have forgotten it or lost it on the day of the action at Oradour-sur-Glane.

« I solemnly declare, that this satchel, made of green fabric, contained :

« 1. A green waterproofed cloth ;

« 2. A Michelin road map on which were pencilled various itineraries with the names of main towns and insertions of dates ;

« 3. 8 postcards, one of which was written by hand and already written out to an address in Germany and another one which hed a date on it ;

« 4. Various letters which I burnt ».

This satchel and contents were handed to us in September 1944.

The map is most suggestive. The S.S. had pencilled in a very clear line the routes they took in our country until their arrival in the department of Limousin. Thanks to this, we could trace their journey from town to town. There were two itineraries :

First itinerary — The first followed by these troops since their appearance in France, crosses the « occupied zone » from north-east

to south-west (from Mulhouse to Bordeaux) starting along the northern section and continuing in the western section of the old
demarcation line. There is no freehand road line and the route only
takes the main roads. It traverses Mulhouse, Belfort, Baume-les-
Dames, Besançon, Dôle, Dijon, Nuits-Saints-Georges, Beaune,
Autun, Château-Chinon, Nevers, Bourges, Vierzon, Villefranche-
sur-Cher, Saint-Aignan, Montrichard, Chenonceaux, Tours, Mont-
bazon, Sainte-Maure, La Celle-Saint-Avant, Châtellerault, Poitiers,
Vivonne, Mansle, Angoulême, Barbezieux, Montlieu, Cavignac,
Saint-André-de-Cubzac and Bordeaux.

Second itinerary — The second, left from Bordeaux and penetrated the so called free zone, following the Garonne as far as Mois-
sac, and then suddenly ascending to the north-east and finally to the
North. On this last section, certain names of towns are boxed or
simply underlined in pencil. Sometimes figures are written alongside, symbols or often even a date.

An examination of this journey shows that the names of towns in
boxes are those of places where the troops billetted. Indeed, the
example of Saint-Junien, where, as we know, they stopped, and which
is also treated on the map in the same way, seems to establish this
quite clearly. The succession of dates written alongside this journey
shows that they could only correspond to the dates of the billetings.
There is decidedly no lack of method or precision in Nazi regiments !

We do not know why certain places have been underlined, nor the
meaning of certain symbols or letters accompanying them. Doubt-
less, some or other of these symbols mark the happening of some
atrocities.

Present communication difficulties prevent us from going further
in obtaining a definite opinion in This matter, but it is well known that
many criminals habitually make a note of the dates of their crimes.

We shall describe this second itinerary boxing in the names of
towns which are boxed on the map followed by the dates of billeting placed alongside. Until Valence-d'Agen.

Team of helpers transporting human remains.

Bordeaux	
Barsac	2-3.
Langon	3-3-44.
Saint-Médard-en-Jalles	S 23-3 = 6-4.
Agen	7-4-44.
Valence	8-4-44.

We can therefore reconstruct this first part of the journey as follows :

Bordeaux, Barsac (on the 2nd March), Langon (on the 3rd March). After Langon they returned to Bordeaux where they stayed until the 23rd and then proceeded to Saint-Médard-en Jalles where there is a large gunpowder factory. They stayed there from 23rd March to 6th April whence they moved into the region of Cahors. In this area, the itinerary contains no further dates, but goes through La Française, Lauzerte, Montcuq and finishes at Cahors.

The S.S. seem to have stayed a month on guerilla activities in the departments of Lot and Aveyron. As the roads they followed crossed and intertwined, it was impossible for us to determine exactly the direction of their executions from this information.

Further east, the itinerary includes names of localities boxed and followed by the dates of billeting. From these details, we may reconstruct the timing of these stages as follows :

Caussade	3-5-44.
Gramat	10-5-44.
Bagnac	11-5-44.
Villecomtal	24-5-44.
Caylus	25-5-44.

A look at the line drawn for this stage shows that during this itinerary, the troops also passed through Figeac, Capdenac, Decazeville and Villefranche-de-Rouergue, probably without billeting there, as these towns were not boxed. It is possible that at that time they used Cahors as a rallying point.

However this may be, they turned up in Frayssinet, whose name is marked with a cross. They seemed to have passed at the end of May in this area.

After Frayssinet, although the journey is marked out with a clear pencil line, no further indication is given of day or month. Nevertheless, a number of names of towns were boxed and underlined. We reproduce the journey below :

| Frayssinet | +, Gourdon, Sarlat, Terrasson, Larche, | Brive |

| Tulle | Masseret, Pierre-Buffière, | Limoges | , | Saint-Junien |

This region visited by the troops after Bordeaux, may be shown to comprise the departments of Lot-et-Garonne, Tarn-et-Garonne, Lot, Aveyron, Corrèze, Dordogne, and Haute-Vienne, i.e. those departments where the Maquis were best established. It is obvious from this that the purpose of these troops was to combat the interior resistance army, but there is no doubt that they preferred to cowardly menace defenceless inhabitants. Thanks to this map, it will be possible to identify the perpetrators of a number of atrocities committed on the population in these areas. For example, we have been able to locate those who executed the killings at Frayssinet.

On the 18th September, 1944, Radio Limoges' 1:30 p.m. programme recounted at length the odious activities for which a detachment of German troops was to blame at Frayssinet. They had a shot a dozen hostages and burnt a certain number of houses. We find in this tragedy, the same cruelty and the same methods as those which were established at Oradour : Here, as there, they killed, burnt and pillaged ; They asserted that there were terrorists in the town, assembled all the inhabitants in the public square and shut

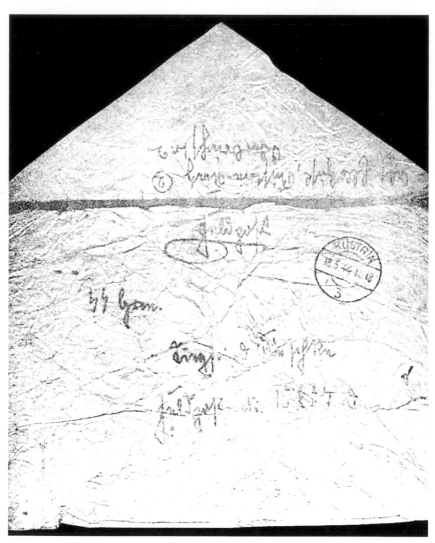

Posted envelope found at Oradour near the corpses of two inhabitants.

Post card found at Oradour in a satchel.

them in the church. But at Frayssinet there was no general massacre as a result of a counter order at the last moment. The unit responsible for the crime was not disclosed, but the method of operation lays the gravest suspicions on, the assassins of Oradour.

The examination of this map particularily strengthens these suppositions since it indicates precisely the period when the S.S. were billeted at Frayssinet, whose name is boxed in pencil. We also noted that on our map, it was marked by a cross. Surely everyone will understand the tragic and eloquent significance attached to the inclusion of this symbol.

Identification of certain S.S. soldiers
responsible for the killing at Oradour, thanks to unedited hand-written documents left by them on the scene of their crime

We have said that the assassins of Oradour left behind several other documents as they withdrew. These, we shall study successively. They are : 1. An envelope posted and addressed to one of them ; 2. One complete postcard and a second damaged, both written on by hand. These documents also allow some of these devilish characters to be named.

POSTED ENVELOPE

In september 1944, Monsieur Sonntag, director of the Nieul Sorting Office in the department of Haute-Vienne, in the presence of Monsieur Léglise, an employee at that place, handed over to us an especially interesting document, a copy of which has been reproduced opposite. It shows the name and address of one of the perpetrators of the massacre of Oradour. It is a yellow envelope bearing the following hand-written address :

S.S. gre. Siegfried Kuschke
Feld Post. N° 15807 D.

The soldier in question is therefore an S.S. grenadier by the name of Siegfried Kuschke. His unit's postal sector is 15807 D.

The envelope was posted in Kustrin, as can be seen from the post mark. The sender's name is also mentioned on the back of the envelope :

Abs Elli. Gusk. Kustrin-Kints (2)

Oderburchstr (2)

Madame Léglise stated that this envelope had been found by her on the 15th June at Oradour-sur-Glane on the road to Les Bordes village next to two corpses lying on the ground who seemed to be men of about 45 and 75 years old respectively.

We have printed a photocopy of this document : the document had been on the ground for five days and the ink was a little washed out but is nevertheless sufficiently legible.

POST CARD

The small military satchel containing the Michelin map furnished by Monsieur Villoutreix and which was considered in a previous section, also contained a picture postcard written on by hand by one of the authors of the killing and showing his name and address. This is reproduced on p. 119. It was part of a pile of a dozen other unused cards depicting a series of photographs of S.S. soldiers in combat. The text, written in gothic handwriting, is quite difficult to decipher.

This card deserves our closest attention, as it allow us, as does the envelope we have just examined, to identify one of the assassins of Oradour. He was S.S. panzer grenadier by the name of Lzipke or Lzupke, being very possibly Polish. Significant is the same postal section number 15807 D as that mentioned on the envelope described above.

This document also furnishes the address of the correspondent of its author, another S.S. soldier belonging to a section bearing the name Ascha. His name is G. Koch and belonged to the 4th S.S.D. at Prag-Krusing S.S. barracks.

FURTHER HANDWRITTEN DOCUMENT

In September 1944, at the Nieul Radio centre, Monsieur Sonntag, in the presence of Monsieur Léglise, handed over to us a fragment of an illustrated post card bearing the following inscription in ink :

S.S. ASCHA
LAUHER
3 S.S. DF.

This document incontestibly furnishes an address : it is that of an S.S. soldier named Lauher of the ASCHA division. The ASCHA name is recognizable to us as having been identified on the post card described above. The name is followed by the code 3 S.S. DF.

This card was found opposite the police station of Nieul on the 11th June, 1944 by Monsieur Michot, from the local sorting office. Does this document supply us with the name and address of one of those responsible for the killing ? We do not think so. It seems rather that it is of a friend of some S.S. soldiers billeted at Nieul. Whatever it may be, we stress that it may be important.

*
**

Firstly, is it certain that the various handwritten documents found at Oradour which we have just described (map, posted envelope and postcard) definitely belonged to an S.S. soldier who shared the responsibility for the detestable crime on the 10th June ? Could they not have been lost in the area by some soldiers who formed part of the camouflage detachment which operated there on the 12th June, which instead of coming from Saint-Junien, had operated out of Limoges and who therefore belonged to the 2nd Batallion of the Der Führer regiment, some of whose reports we shall publish hereafter ?

This hypothesis is far from verified by the facts :

We have seen that the envelope on the one hand, and the postcard on the other hand, which were found at Oradour both bear references to the postal sector 15807 D. Now it has been established that this postal sector was that of the contingent billeted at Saint-Junien. We have seen this, indeed, on the pass issued by the officer in command of the unit : 15807 D (Dienstelle) (see page 21). It is also known that the postal sector of the unit from Limoges that issued the reports we have just spoken about, is 59731 B (dienstselle) (see page 122).

If any other argument were required, we would only have to refer to the map with its markings as mentioned above. It is clear in fact that the final place in the itinerary followed by its owner, i.e. the last stage, is indeed that of Saint-Junien. The name of the locality is also boxed around, showing that they were billeted there.

There is no doubt whatsoever that the S.S. who mislaid these three documents formed part of the troops of Saint-Junien and not of that of Limoges.

Causes of the massacre at Oradour

and contribution to the identification
of the division responsible
according to unedited German military reports.

We have the good fortune to be in a position to publish two reports, the importance of which will not escape the reader's mind. Both of them were drawn up by the 19th S.S. police regiment, the first on the 13th June, 1944, and the second on the 17th June, 1944, i.e. after the massacre at Oradour.

We must first mention that the commander of this battallion was major Aboth of the Schutzpolizei, his second in command being Hauptmann Engelbrecht of the Schutzpolizei. This unit was placed at Marceau barracks in Limoges, the regiment command being at Lyon.

We shall give the essential elements of these two reports plus their translations and consider them one at a time.

FIRST REPORT

II/S. S. Pol. Rgt 19   O. U., den 13/6/1944
    la - 1105/44
Tgb. Nr. 180/44 (g)

Lagebericht
für die Zeit vom 16.5. — 14.6.1944

I. *Allgemeine Lage :*

....

Eine vor‚bergehende Aktion der S.S. Panzerdivision « Das Reich » in Limoges und Umgebung, hat auf die Bevölkerung sichtbaren Eindruck gemacht.

A brief action of the S.S. Panzerdivision « Das Reich » at Limoges and surrounding area made a visible impression on the population.

SECOND REPORT

Dienststelle   O. U., den 17/6/1944.
Feldpostnummer 59.731 B.
  5/S. S. - Pol. Rgt 19.

Betr. Beitrag zum Zustandsbericht.

....

Der Beginn der Vergeltungsmaßnahmen hat ein merkbares Aufatmen hervorgerufen und die stimmung sehr günstig beeinflubt.

« Morale — The commencement of reprisals has brought about a favourable improvement in the morale of the troops, who are now noticeably more at ease ».

The first report, emanating from the commander of the second batallion, indicates that detachments from this unit were sent several times to combat the « bandits » of the Limoges region and emphasizes the impression This had on the population. This document confirms the conclusions we have just made after studying the map found at Oradour, namely that the S.S. travelling through Limousin had, as their brief, the removal of members of the Maquis and the implementation of punitive expeditions against the inhabitants. It gives an account of the favourable results obtained in order to justify the actions.

Noting that this report was drawn up on the 13th June, 1944, i.e. three days after the massacre of Oradour, it is understandable that its purpose was to justify the massacre by mentioning the importance of the advantages which the Reich had gained from it.

The second report was drawn up under the direction of Krafstaffel (automobile) commander, ob. It Jaenich, whose second-in-command was ob. It Krause.

This document, written on the 17th June, 1944, i.e. one week after the atrocities at Oradour, attempts, as does the previous report, to justify them but whereas the first speaks of the effects produced on the minds of the local people, the latter raises the matter of its salutary influence on the troop's morale.

But can it really be called an army if it needs such crimes in order to lift its morale ? We may tremble at the thought of crimes that it could have done if it had gained victory or simply if it had been given time.

These reports also irrefutably prove that the atrocities which they gave themselves over to committing, in particular the killing at Oradour, were both designed and ordered by the commanders. They congratulated themselves on the results obtained, though it might mean later disowning the officer who commanded « the operation ». If need be, they will pretend that he was shot by the firing squad whilst in reality he would have been given a promotion.

Finally, let us note that the « commencement of reprisals » referred to in this document, constitutes an undisguised promise of new killings in the entire Limousin region ; the sudden call up to the Normandy front of most of the regiments specialised in this sort of

« expedition » was the only thing to interrupt the flow of their monstrous doings.

These two reports illustrate with utmost clarity the state of mind of the « Great Reich » the day after the landings. Newspaper, radio and cinema propaganda, assisted by propaganda from the notorious collaborators of the occupied countries, always tried to make believe that the Nazi military capability was strong enough to prevent any invasion of the « subjugated nations ». But the S.S. ; who were no doubt bombarded with similar propaganda, must have been seething with rage to learn of the success of the Normandy landings at the same time as being called up to that front. The Panzer division, known as « Das Reich », the elite reprisal force, wanted to make an example before leaving the areas where the unassailable and feared Maquis were struggling ceaselessly for the liberation of the country.

That is how, by terrifying the population by a crime unprecedented in history, they thought to cover their rears and » favourably improve the troop's morale » by increasing its awareness of its own strength by assassinating defenceless populations !

Such a psychological error could only have been committed by the children of a people long since reduced to slavery and which had submitted its individual faculty of judgement to that of its leaders.

This was its downfall.

OTHER GERMAN REPORTS

Various other reports drawn up between on the 3rd April and on the 13th June, 1944 establish that this second battallion was operating against the Maquis :

1. In the region of Tulle (night of 31st March to 1st April, 1944) ;
2. At Saint-Junien, on the 18th May, 1944 ;
3. At La Péritie, on the 5th and 6th June, 1944 ;
4. At La Souterraine, on the 8th and 9th June, 1944

The formation which was at La Péritie on the 5th and 6th June and at La Souterraine on the 8th and 9th June was therefore fully operational in the region of Limousin on the 10th June, 1944, i.e. the day of the action at Oradour. It could be supposed that they had participated in it.

But if the troops who brawled at La Péritie and at La Souterraine were the same as those who fought at Tulle on the night of the 31st March to 1st April, 1944 and at Saint-Junien on the 18th May, 1944, it would seem impossible to identify these with those of Oradour.

Indeed, if we refer to the calendar created from our itinerary map, it can be seen that during the night of the 31st March to 1st April, the troops we are concerned with were still in the region of Bordeaux, to be precise at Saint-Médard-en-Jalles, and that on the 18th May they were involved in operations near Bagnac and Villecomtal.

What was the division in question at Oradour ?

Two points may be clearly established :

1. The division which « operated » in Limousin was the « Das Reich » division. The reports cited above are quite explicit in this regard ;

2. The S.S. soldiers who committed the crime at Oradour belonged to the « Der Führer » regiment. We have shown that they were part of the same unit as those who were billetted at Rochechouard and we have ourselves established that on the lower sleeve of the tunic of one of those soldiers, there was a very noticable padded band bearing he words « Der Führer ». Now at Oradour, this item of clothing was covered by a kind of cloth jacket which prevented the inscription from being noticed.

It would seem that the troops who committed the atrocities of Oradour, according to information given by the map studies above, were only in Limousin since the end of May and were under the central command of the « Das Reich » division at Limoges. We hasten to add that it is not improbable to believe that elements barracked there were able to accompany them in their execution of the killing at Oradour and, in particular, that the commander of the « Kraftstaffel » (automobile) had supplied some of the vehicles necessary in the circumstances.

We also know that the S.S. from Oradour and those from Limoges were in close liaison. We supply a very telling statement in this regard.

Testimony establishing the existence of a liaison between the S.S. involved in Oradour and certain units from Limoges

Madame Marie Loustaud, 57, who lives near Veyrac station four kilometres from Oradour-sur-Glane, stated that on the 10th June at about 7 p.m. she saw two German automobiles coming from Oradour and travelling in the direction of Limoges. She saw them coming back to Oradour at about 8 p.m. the same evening.

It is of course possible to know whether they were carrying soldiers going to give an account of the results of the expedition of Oradour, or to look for orders, or even whether they went to load special machinery or munitions. They nevertheless demonstrated that theirs was a link which is important to be aware of between the S.S. « Der Führer » division in operation at Oradour and the S.S. occupying or stationed at Limoges (S.S. « Das reich » division)

Now that we have ascertained the division and regiment which the unit responsible for Oradour belonged to, it remains for us to identify its company. This will be the subject of the following section.

Evidence from moral inscriptions
of the company number of the S.S. in question at Oradour

We found at Nieul a piece of evidence which we are bound to disclose. The S.S. at Oradour, as we have seen, were billeted at Nieul

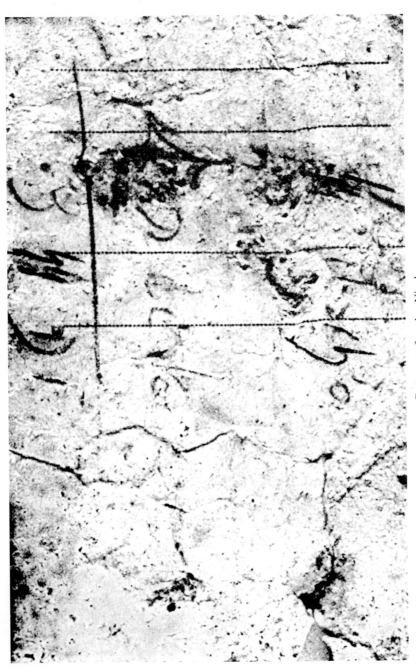

Document found at Nieul.

on the evening of their crime. A group of them occupied the school building. No one in the area has any doubt that the unit that stayed there was indeed the unit that had just burned the martyred town. We have many detailed proofs of this. The new bicycle which belonged to Monsieur Barthèlemy, of Oradour-sur-Glane, and the motor scooter of Monsieur Leblanc, who lived in the same area, were both abandoned in Nieul by S.S. soldiers and are consequently by no means the least of such proofs.

Two mural inscriptions were discovered at Nieul after the departure of the German troops, one in the town school, the other in the house of Monsieur Rivet, a pharmacist.

1. *Inscription at the school* — The headmaster of the school, Monsieur Bouty, showed us on the wall containing the doors of the two boys school classrooms some writing in chalk which we reproduce as follows :

16 man

3 KP.

The word « man » is incomplete so that the next must be translated as follows : 16 men 3rd company.

The letters KP are an abbreviation for the latter word. We requested the headmaster to ensure that these two inscriptions be preserved.

2. *Inscription at the chemist* — The following inscription in chalk, was noticed by Monsieur Rivet on two doors to separate rooms on the first floor of his chemist's shop.

Fisrt door : 4 S. Scha.

3 KP.

Second door : 7 S. Scha.

3 KP.

These inscriptions were written on the afternoon of the 9th June, 1944 by a German sub-officer accompanied by an interpreter who spoke French well. The two men woke Monsieur Rivet during the night of the 10th June, 1944 to ask him to show them the way to

Chamboret. This inscription and the one at the school irrefutably demonstrate that the 3rd company was the one at Oradour.

*
**

As we have seen, the various evidence supplied in our documentation has enabled us to establish the causes of the monstrous massacre of Oradour, to discover the division, regiment and company of those who bear such awesome responsibility, to know where the unit came from and even to identify some of the abominable assassins.

At the time of going to press, the bright sun of victory has just dissipated this sombre, tragic night of our poor country's occupation. Our emotions go out to Oradour's martyrs ! These are the words of General de Gaulle when he came to pay tribute at their tombs : « Oradour-sur-Glane is the symbol of the evils that have befallen our country. Their memory must be remembered since such an evil must never be repeated ».

In honour of Oradour's martyrs

On Friday the 16th June, 1944, Monseigneur the Bishop of Limoges gave the following address at the cathedral :

« It is my duty to inform my diocese that I have expressed my painful indignation to the commander general of the occupation forces at Limoges because of the dessecration of the church at Oradour-sur-Glane by the execution within its walls of hundreds of women, young girls and children and its profanation by the destruction of the tabernacle and the removal of the holy eucharist and I have demanded that an enquiry be called with the purpose of ensuring that justice and honour is done.

« My dear brothers and sisters, let us first pray for the souls of the hundreds of victims, men, including three of our priests, women and children who were pushed to tragically and so suddenly towards their eternity on the 10th June. De Profundis.

« Let us then pray for the numerous families in mourning, most for more than one victim. Our father, Hail Mary.

« Finally, let us request God's pardon for the double sacrilege for the spilling of blood in the holy place and for the profanation of the holy eucharist. Spare us O Lord ».

*
**

On the 18th June, 1944, Pastor Chaudier, currently president of the departmental liberation committee, gave the following sermon in the prostestant church of Limoges :

« First and foremost, we honour all these dead. Perhaps among them, there were some, young or adult, who came from our churches, but this is of no matter. We salute them all with respect, with pain, with tenderness. Among so many, many civilian victims of this vilifying war, it is understandable that by linking them closely to that numberless crowd of innocents, as they, who went before them to eternity, we should want to make a special place for them. With more terrifying refinements than many others and to a degree unequalled hitherto to our knowledge, in the country of France, their end was an unspeakable martyrdom. We salute all these dead so close to us only by the distance of their poor tomb, yet far closer still in our broken hearts. We do not seek to join ourselves to their poor remains, mixed together in the charred tomb that was a church, by too saddening a description ; we shall join with their souls in the invisible, where they shall at last be promoted to that inviolate freedom of the children of God and we shall commit them to the love of Him who extends his two crucified arms over the indescribable carnage. Upon all these sacrificed ones and, in their name, upon all those who must replace them in the exhausted France of tomorrow, we shall invoke the Spirit who propagates saving memories, who brings to birth harvest of goodness, of justice and of peace out of bloody holocausts and by whom the dead become builders, side by side with the living, of creations to come.

« The horror that was so spilled out over a small town in our belo-
ved Limousin, impells us towards another duty than that of rende-
ring homage to victims or weeping over them. The human conscience and the Christian conscience are one in standing against
other such killing ».

Conclusion

We have been as objective as possible in recounting this horrific
crime.

It could not be said that such cruelty was the particular act of soldiers more criminal than others, brought together under exceptional
circumstances. In Dordogne, Charente, Corrèze, Haute-Vienne,
only to speak of our own region, we have stopped counting the
number of towns and villages set on fire. Everywhere, hosteges are
slaughtered. At Brantôme, Rouffignac, Terrasson and Chabanais.

The excuse was given that when they set fire to Oradour-sur-
Glane, the S.S. had mistaken the name and that it was the town of
Oradour-sur-Vayres that they intended to let themselves loose upon.
For some people, it is this small town in which we live, also close
to Oradour, which was to suffer this tragic end. Indeed, several
expeditions were tried against this town and it was several times
necessary to flee, not forgetting besides, to hide in our gardens,
those objects we were too weak to let go.

That is why the documents which we are presenting today to the
public, yes, indeed, this manuscript, remained buried for several
days under a lawn.

We hasten to say that it is thanks to the courageous troops of the
French Interior Force that our town was always preserved.

This crime gives such a strong impression of having been prepared, developed and thought out that it seems to us impossible that a
mistake of this sort could have happened.

What is most striking when the circumstances of the terrible crime of Oradour are examined, is the methodical, systematic and even scientific manner in which it was perpetrated. The whole thing was studied in general and in detail, conceived with an alarming luxury of precautions and executed with cruelty and disconcerting refinement. The authors of these monstrosities acted in complete unity, as if they were carrying out some simple and everyday excercise. For example, they primordially established a command post, an exact count of the victims was kept, the men and women were separated and the men were lined up on the market square in rows of three. Everything was anticipated. Tracker vehicles were included in the convoy in order to cross over farm land so as to chase any inhabitants. A shot fired from the market square was the signal for the execution, a measure to prevent any groups aroused by the first shootings to panic and revolt. The German insistence in asking whether there were any munitions dumps was evidently a step of prudence which may be explained by the desire to protect against any explosions which the fire might cause and of which they might be the first victims. The pillage was carefully organised and, as we have seen, no door was to be left looked. All the equipment and material necessary to light the inferno was there : bombs, cartridges, incendiary bombs ; the last word in science and progress ! An asphyxiating gas container intended for the liquidation of the unfortunate victims in the church was specially brought in by lorry. Everything was studied, prepared knowledgeably and with due precaution. One eloquent proof of this may be seen in the following instance : a house situated near the town, belonging to F… and of whom we have already had occasion to speak, was not set on fire, because it was situated on the other side of the sign which delimits the town of Oradour-sur-Glane.

Those in the house were also spared. They nevertheless had to stay in their home and a machine-gun was trained on their door all the time the killing lasted.

Hitler's beast acted everywhere on orders and according to tasks as received.

We had all been warned a long time before by certain sections of the occupation forces themselves that in the event that they found themselves under the obligation to evacuate our country, they would not fail to devote themselves to implacable acts of barbarism.

It is no longer possible to speak of a German army. Our charming and peaceful countryside of France has been rifled by pillaging bands who burn our towns and savagely assassinate its inhabitants. The Germans have distinguished themselves from other peoples by their delirious taste for torture, death and blood.

In his funeral speech over the victims of the killing at Oradour, the ex-prefect of Haute-Vienne cried out : « The French language does not possess strong enough words to describe this act ». It is true that the unleashing of such monstrous instincts and the obsession with atrocities such as these has no name in any language – except however in the German language, where the term « Schadenfreude » has been created and which may be translated as pleasure in doing evil. How edifying it is when we find that in Germany such a brutal state of mind, heart and spirit should be so natural, normal and usual that it should be necessary to create a special word to designate this !

The race of Lords tried to impose upon us the benefits of Germans Kultur ; the resplendent, superior, fertile and eternal Kultur with, as its sweetest fruits, the S.S.

In our country, its consecration was sought by complete application of its scientific method to all acts of existence, by the progressive subjugation of the will, the desires, the preferences and the instincts ! It was the codification of all virtues, all feelings, the stark mathematics of beauty, good and truth, yes, those illusory and sterile regulations, that empty and excessive discipline and it was consequently work, then feast, then pleasures, in that very particular order, mass produced obligations, standardised consciences and finally happiness obligatory for everyone with enthusiasm to order and joy on command. « Strength through joy », as they proclaim in a well-known slogan. Well-known, yes, and celebrated ! Strength through joy ! And joy... through strength !

17-12-44

The ruins of the church (sketch by M. Guy Pauchou).

Some of the survivors

In front : the young Roger Godfrin, aged 8, who hid so as not to go to the gathering. He is the only child who was at school on this day (when there should have been a medical inspection) and who escaped the killing.

First row, left to right : Senon Armand, Borie Mathieu, Senon Daniel[1], Broussaudier Clément, Beaubreuil Joseph, Besson Robert, Doutre Paul, Machefer Martial.

Second row, left to right : Roby Yvon, Darthout Marcel, Beaubreuil Maurice, Désourteaux Hubert, Renaud Aimé.

Missing from the photo : Brissaud Martial, Bélivier Marcel, Garraud, Hébras Robert, Redon Hippolyte, Mlles Pinède, his brother, Rénaud Jeanine.

---

1. The postman was on his rounds.

The Bordeaux Trial

On January 12, 1953 the trial begins after a procedure that has been going on for nearly nine years.

Difficult procedure, lack of proofs, responsible men missing and of course amnesia of all the accused members.

Out of sixty-five men being identified, twenty-one are present, most of them being free defendants. There are 7 germans including a sergeant. All of them being men in the evil division Das Reich. Not one officer ! Commander Dickman died in Normandy. Captain Kahn « disappeared » in Sweden. General Lammerding resumed his job in Düsseldorf. He could not be reached in the British occupied zone. He even sent a letter to the Court to justify his men's conduct : they were complying with orders. As for lieutenant Barth be will be « discovered » only 37 years later in East Germany living a happy life.

From the biginning of the trial there is a fight in the procedure. Will the French Alsatians be tried at the same time as the Germans ? The court says « yes » but trouble goes on during the hearings.

M. Brouillaud, chairman of the Association of the Families of the Martyrs of Oradour the leader of the delegation of the witnesses and the victim's relatives. They look dignified in their distress. They show no hatred, they cry for justice.

Then comes the indictment, never ending... trying to describe the horror. Then the witnesses, the escapees come in their turn to describe their pain still burning nine years later ? They describe the plundering before the fire, the organised massacre of 642 men, women and children, often burnt alive.

The accused. In this atmosphere of horror, they stay cool, waiting, they show no compassion on their victim's parents' tears. As if the trial wasn't their trial. Besides, they don't remenber. They were on guard. If they shot, they did not aim at anyone.

February 13, 1953, the Court returns a verdict, first the Germans, the sergeant major is sentenced to death. The others : one is discharged, 5 are condemned to ten and twelve years in prison. The Alsatian sergeant in sentenced to death, the other thirteen are condemned to five or eight years in prison.

This trial doesn't please anyone. In Oradour, people are overwhelmed, disgusted. The families grieve in spite of sympathy shown to them in Limousin.

In Alsace some newspapers support the « enrolled by force ». These reactions influence members of Parliement who in the name of Unity vote amnesty on February 21, discharging the 13 Alsatians who had been condemned.

On that very day they leave prison free, together with six German soldiers who had served their sentence.

Oradour gave back to the State the Cross of the Legion of Honour and the Military Cross that had been presented a few years earlier, and was opposed to the transfer of the victim's ashes to the ossuary built by the State and so built a tomb in the communal cemetary.

The Berlin trial.

Lieutenant Barth had been living in R.D.A. in his native village under his name until 1981 not being troubled. It is during the cold war that the service for research of war criminals finally found him without excessive ardour but perhaps political reasons may be the basis for this discovery.

A last the trial, begins in East Berlin on May 25, 1983.

The delegation of witnesses for Oradour includes five escapee : MM. Hebras, Roby, Machefer, Beaubreuil and Darthout. They relate that afternoon of June 10, 1944 when a detachment of the division Das Reich exterminated 642 victims and destroyed the village of Oradour. They discribe the horror permanently on their minds and hearts 40 years later.

Barth admits everything.

No, there were no weapons in Oradour. No underground mouvement. Orders have been given by Commander Dickman. The village was to be destroyed with the inhabitants including women and children. No regret. He had not throught about it, he had obeyed. During a war one follows strictly the rules.

Verdict : maximun penalty, life imprisonment.

Lieutenant Barth was condemned to life imprisonment on the 7th June 1983... Old and ill, he was released in 1997.

The Berlin wall collapsed six years later in 1989.

LIST OF PEOPLE WHOSE CORPSES HAVE BEEN IDENTIFIED AND FOR WHOM DEATH CERTIFICATES HAVE BEEN ISSUED

NUMBER	NAME AND CHRISTIAN NAME	PROFESSION	DATE OF BIRTH	PLACE OF RESIDENCE
1	Mme Thomas (Mathilde), née Ragon	Unemployed	In 1898, La Chapelle-Thémer (Vendée)	Oradour-sur-Glane.
2	Thomas (Marcelin)	Baker	In 1892, Peyrilhac	Oradour-sur-Glane.
3	Poutaraud (Pierre-Henri)	Car mechanic	16th June 1911, Chaptelat (H.-V.)	Oradour-sur-Glane.
4	Desbordes (Marie), née Ribette	Farmer	30th January 1901, Saint-Brice (H.-V.)	Chez Magnaud, Oradour-sur-Glane.
5	Chalard (Marcelin)	Electrician	17th April 1888, Aixe-sur-Vienne	11, rue d'Aixe, Limoges.
6	D'Albois (Pierre)		10th February 1923, Sonzay (I.-et-L.)	11, rue de Courville, Orléans.
7	Dupic (Léonard), dit Pierre	Unemployed	28th October 1867, Peyrilhac	Oradour-sur-Glane.
8	Mme Joyeux (Henriette), née Hyvernaud		22nd September 1921, Chamboret (H.-V.)	Soudanas, commune de Panazol.
9	Widow Mme Dalstein (Octavie), née Bertrand		24th April 1877, Sainte-Barbe (Moselle)	Oradour-sur-Glane.
10	Avril (Michel-Henri)	Timber merchant	6th January 1907, Cieux (H.-V.)	Oradour-sur-Glane.
11	Joyeux (René)		24th November 1943, Limoges	Soudanas, commune de Panazol.

12	Mme Milord (Hélène), née Brun	Clerk	9th August 1917, Saint-Junien (H.-V.)	77, faubourg Montjovis, Limoges.
13	Widow Mme Trouillaud (Catherine-Marie), née Raynaud		7th January 1890, Oradour-sur-Glane	Oradour-sur-Glane
14	Sadry (Jean)		12th February 1932, Saint-Martin-de-Jussac	Le Repaire, Oradour-sur-Glane
15	Aliotti (Christiane)		21st July 1940, Toulon (Var)	Oradour-sur-Glane
16	Raymond (Pierre)	Farmer	9th August 1873, Saint-Martin-de-Jussac	Valeix, Oradour-sur-Glane
17	Duvernet (François)	Smallholder	26th September 1898, Oradour-sur-Glane	Chez Penot, Oradour-sur-Glane
18	Courivaud (Maurice)	Butcher	13th November 1920, Paris (13e)	La-Tuilière-des-Bordes, Oradour-sur-Glane
19	Tessaud (Jean)	Tanner	22nd February 1890, Saint-Martin-de-Jussac	2, rue Beauclair, Saint-Junien.
20	Désourteaux (Jean-Paul)	Doctor	7th September 1872, Oradour-sur-Glane	Oradour-sur-Glane
21	Villoutreix (Henri)	Day labourer	13th November 1899, Oradour-sur-Glane	Les Carderies, Oradour-sur-Glane
22	Mme Hyvernaud (Germaine-Marie), née Bois	Farmer	24th September 1903, Peyrilhac (H.-V.)	Oradour-sur-Glane

NUMBER	NAME AND CHRISTIAN NAME	PROFESSION	DATE OF BIRTH	PLACE OF RESIDENCE
23	Thomas (Raymond)		26th June 1932, Oradour-sur-Glane	Les Bordes, Oradour-sur-Glane
24	Thomas (Georges)		17th July 1930, Oradour-sur-Glane	Les Bordes, Oradour-sur-Glane
25	Widow Mme Devoyon (Françoise), née Chevalier		10th October 1866, Chamboret (H.-V.)	Oradour-sur-Glane
26	Morliéras (Lucien)	Hairdresser	29th October 1902, Veyrac	Oradour-sur-Glane
27	Lachaud (Léonard)	Bricklayer	26th September 1872, Oradour-sur-Glane	Les Bordes, Oradour-sur-Glane
28	Milord (françois)	Assistant Supplies Corps	16th February 1915, Oradour-sur-Glane	16, rue de la Convention, Oullins (Rhône).
29	Besson (Guillaume)	Fabric merchant	1st November 1882, Collandres (Cantal)	Oradour-sur-Glane
30	Joyeux (Antonin)	Pit sawyer	23rd August 1904, Oradour-sur-Glane	Oradour-sur-Glane
31	Lacroix (Jean)	Farmer	28st July 1909, Oradour-sur-Glane	Puy Gaillard, Oradour-sur-Glane
32	Vialette (Michèle)		31st July 1939, Oradour-sur-Glane	Oradour-sur-Glane

33	Vialette (Danielle)		10th October 1941, Oradour-sur-Glane	Oradour-sur-Glane
34	Foussat (Marie-Léon) dit André	Miller	24th October 1905, Oradour-sur-Glane	Le Repaire, Oradour-sur-Glane
35	Roumy (Jean)		24th June 1896, Peyrilhac	Oradour-sur-Glane
36	Hyvernaud (Marcel)		2nd April 1936, Oradour-sur-Glane	Mazenty, Oradour-sur-Glane
37	Pinède (Robert)		25th July 1899, Oloron-Saint-Marie (B.-P.)	Oradour-sur-Glane
38	Valentin (Jean)		23rd September 1884, Bussière-Galant	Oradour-sur-Glane
39	Bardet (Léonard)		15th March 1880, Peyrilhac	Oradour-sur-Glane
40	Chapelot (Louis-Léonard)		5th September 1900, Oradour-sur-Glane	Oradour-sur-Glane
41	Nicolas (Jean-Baptiste)		20th August 1884, Oradour-sur-Glane	Oradour-sur-Glane
42	Moreau (Pierre)		1st August 1885, Aixe-sur-Vienne	Oradour-sur-Glane
43	Raynaud (Henri-Pierre)		19th July 1909, Oradour-sur-Glane	Oradour-sur-Glane
44	Jakobowicz (Sarah)		13th Febuary 1929, Kalich (Pologne)	Oradour-sur-Glane
45	Moreau (Lucien)		8th January 1911, Javerdat	18, rue de la Brasserie, Limoges.

NUMBER	NAME AND CHRISTIAN NAME	PROFESSION	DATE OF BIRTH	PLACEOF RESIDENCE
46	Lavergne (Jean-Baptiste)		23rd December 1902, Cieux	21, rue du Clos-Augier, Limoges
47	Lavergne (Jean)		5th October 1926, Cieux	Oradour-sur-Glane
48	Peyroulet (Marcel-Léon)		26th December 1911, La Roche-l'Abeille (H.-V.)	La Betoulle, commune de Blond, Haute-Vienne
49	Jackow (Jean)		15th October 1905, Siedliska (Pologne)	Le Mas-ferrat, Oradour-sur-Glane
50	Mirablon (Albert)		1st March 1909, Paterson (Etats-Unis)	6, rue Orphéroux, Limoges
51	Chabaudon (Maurice)		1st January 1914, Limoges	81, avenue Garibaldi, Limoges
52	Tournier (Jean-Baptiste)		29th May 1893, Limoges.	Rue Buffon, Limoges

LIST OF NAMES OF THE VICTIMS OF THE MASSACRE IN ORADOUR-SUR-GLANE THE 10TH JUNE 1944 OFFICIALLY DECLARED MISSING

NUMBER	NAME AND CHRISTIAN NAME	PROFESSION	DATE OF BIRTH	PLACE OF RESIDENCE
1	Aimond Monique		14th november 1932, Paris 18ᵉ	11, rue Guillaume-Tell, Paris 17ᵉ
2	Alamone (Marie-Louise)	Housemaid	22nd September 1926, Saint-Priest-Taurion	Les Trois-Arbres, Oradour-sur-Glane
3	Aliotti (Michèle)		14th April 1944, Oradour-sur-Glane	Oradour-sur-Glane
4	Aliotti (Félix)	Staff sergent	1st Juiller 1915, Le Kef (Tunisie)	Oradour-sur-Glane
5	Aliotti (Marie)		26th September 1942, Avignon	Oradour-sur-Glane
6	Widow Mᵐᵉ Roumy (Catherine) née Aliphat	Farmer	22nd August 1874, Saint-Gence	Les Brandes, Oradour-sur-Glane
7	Mᵐᵉ Lorrain (Marie) née André		7th Januaryr 1883, Charly	Oradour-sur-Glane
8	Andrieux (Marie), veuve Villoutreix	Unemployed	22nd November 1863, Oradour-sur-Glane	Les Bordes, Oradour-sur-Glane
9	Arnaud (Monique)		24th January 1935, Paris 14ᵉ	Les Bordes, Oradour-sur-Glane
10	Avril (Georges)		20th September 1943, Oradour-sur-Glane	Oradour-sur-Glane
11	Mᵐᵉ Leclerc (Anna) née Audevard	Hairdresser	7th March 1909, Séreilhac	27, faubourg d'Angoulême, Limoges

No.	Name	Occupation	Date and place of birth	Residence
12	Widow Mᵐᵉ Mercier (Jeanne), née Auzannet		29th September 1867, Peyreilhac	Puygaillard, Oradour-sur-Glane
13	Ballot (Jean)	Bricklayer	21st June 1879, Veyrac	Les Bordes, Oradour-sur-Glane
14	Ballot (André)	Notary's clerk	24th December 1928, Oradour-sur-Glane	Les Bordes, Oradour-sur-Glane
15	Ballot (Aimée)		14th Febuary 1932, Oradour-sur-Glane	Les Bordes, Oradour-sur-Glane
16	Mᵐᵉ Boissou (Marie), née Barataud	Farmer	17th August 1899, Oradour-sur-Glane	Le Mas de l'Arbre, Oradour-sur-Glane
17	Mᵐᵉ Villatte (Mélanie), née Bardet	Clerk	18th May 1895, Cieux	Oradour-sur-Glane
18	Bardet (Arthur)	Farmer	1st October 1910, Oradour-sur-Glane	Villa "André", Oradour-sur-Glane
19	Bardet (Gisèle)		4th Febuary 1936, Oradour-sur-Glane	Villa "André", Oradour-sur-Glane
20	Bardet (Daniel)		20th March 1938, Oradour-sur-Glane	Oradour-sur-Glane
21	Widow Mᵐᵉ Lathière (Marie), née Bardet	Cleaning woman	7th September 1894, Oradour-sur-Glane	Oradour-sur-Glane
22	Mᵐᵉ Machefer (Anna), née Bardet	Unemployed	1st January 1913, Oradour-sur-Glane	Oradour-sur-Glane
23	Bardet (Denise)	Teacher	10th June 1920, Verneuil	La Grange-de-Bœil, Veyrac

NUMBER	NAME AND CHRISTIAN NAME	PROFESSION	DATE OF BIRTH	PLACE OF RESIDENCE
24	Bardet (Hubert)		4th August 1937, Oradour-sur-Glane	Oradour-sur-Glane
25	Bardet (André)		4th January 1940, Oradour-sur-Glane	Oradour-sur-Glane
26	Bardet (René)		31st January 1944, Oradour-sur-Glane	Oradour-sur-Glane
27	Bardet (Arsène)		9th March 1935, Oradour-sur-Glane	Oradour-sur-Glane
28	Bardet (Louis)	Carpenter	20th April 1902, Cieux	Oradour-sur-Glane
29	Bardet (André)	Carpenter	3rd December 1924, Chamboret	Oradour-sur-Glane
30	Bardet (Robert)		15th Febuary 1931, Oradour-sur-Glane	Oradour-sur-Glane
31	Widow Mme Pidance (Françoise), née Bariant	Unemployed	14th April 1882, Oradour-sur-Glane	Oradour-sur-Glane
32	Mme Doire (Marguerite), née Bariant	Unemployed	2nd Novembre 1875, Oradour-sur-Glane	Oradour-sur-Glane
33	Barny (Lucien)		28th December 1938, Oradour-sur-Glane	Mazenty, Oradour-sur-Glane
34	Barrière (Marcel)	Mechanic	16th October 1923, Limoges	6, rue de la Cité, Limoges

	Name	Occupation	Birth	Residence
35	Barthélemy (Roger)	Student	10th June 1925, Paris (18e)	Oradour-sur-Glane
36	Barthélemy (Alfred)	Painting contractor	17th Marseille 1887, Marseille	Oradour-sur-Glane
37	Mme Denis (Lucie), née Bayon	Unemployed	7th June 1886, La Chapelle-Taillefer (Creuse)	Oradour-sur-Glane
38	Beau (Jean)	Servant	10th May 1882, Cieux	Cieux
39	Mme Desourteaux (Alice), née Beau	Shopkeeper	27th May1904, Oradour-sur-Glane	Oradour-sur-Glane
40	Beau (Joseph)	Dealerr	7th December 1870, Bellac	Oradour-sur-Glane
41	Widow Mme Milord (Léontine), née Beaubelicout	Hardware dealer	30th October 1887, Javerdat	Oradour-sur-Glane
42	Beaubreuil (Emile)	Carpenter	9th July 1898, Oradour-sur-Glane	Oradour-sur-Glane
43	Mme Mercier (Jeanne), née Beaubreuil	Shopkeeper	12th June 1894, Saint-Victurnien	Oradour-sur-Glane
44	Widow Mme Bassens (Maria), née Beaubreuil	Day labourer	9th March 1886, Oradour-sur-Glane	Oradour-sur-Glane
45	Beaudet (Angèle)	Glover	24th May 1921, Oradour-sur-Glane	Le Vignaud, Oradour-sur-Glane
46	Beaudet (Jean)	Concrete maker	22nd September 1887, Cieux	Le Vignaud, Oradour-sur-Glane
47	Mme Sauviat (Marguerite), née Beaudout	Dressmaker	7th November 1891, Limoges	15, rue du Mas-Loubier, Limoges
48	Beaulieu (Jean-Baptiste)	Smith	22nd December 1884, Oradour-sur-Glane	Oradour-sur-Glane

NUMBER	NAME AND CHRISTIAN NAME	PROFESSION	DATE OF BIRTH	PLACE OF RESIDENCE
49	Belivier (André)	Farmer	17th January 1892, Saint-Auvent	Les Brégères, Oradour-sur-Glane
50	Belivier (Alice)	Farmer	1st September 1923, Oradour-sur-Glane	Les Brégères, Oradour-sur-Glane
51	Belivier (Marie-Louise)	Farmer	3rd September 1930, Oradour-sur-Glane	Les Bregères, Oradour-sur-Glane
52	Bergeron (Jules)	Pensioner	22nd August 1875, Chateaulin (Finistère)	Saint-Venant (Pas-de-Calais)
53	Bergmann (Joseph)		6th Febuary 1917, Ikem (Allemagne)	Oradour-sur-Glane
54	Bergmann (Serge)		5th August 1935, Strasbourg	Oradour-sur-Glane
55	Bertrand (Françoise)		30th March 1930, Clouange (Moselle)	Oradour-sur-Glane
56	Beyne (Claudine)		23rd July 1937, Paris (18e)	Mazenty, Oradour-sur-Glane
57	Bichaud (Jean)	Tailor	28th September 1891, Cieux	38, avenue des Ruchoux, Limoges
58	Bichaud (Pierre)	Turner	6th August 1921, Saint-Brice	Rue du Clos-Jargot, Limoges
59	Bichaud (Léonard)	Road menderr	2nd September 1897, Cieux	Oradour-sur-Glane

No.	Name	Occupation	Date & place of birth	Address
60	Bichaud (Jean-Aimé)		9th July 1934, Oradour-sur-Glane	Les Trois-Arbres, Oradour-sur-Glane
61	Binet (Jean)	Chief technician	15th November 1910, Pontgibaut, P.-de-D.	Faubourg d'Angoulême, Limoges
62	Binet (Jean-Pierre)		13th April 1937, Limoges	Oradour-sur-Glane
63	Mme Roumy (Jean), née Blanchon (Marie)	Unemployed	27th November 1898, Javerdat	Oradour-sur-Glane
64	Blandin (Charles)	Unemployed	17th Octoberr 1886, Maubeuge	Oradour-sur-Glane
65	Bois (Madeleine)		29th November 1935, Bellac	Orbagnac, Oradour-sur-Glane
66	Mme Desroches (Maria), née Boissière	Housewife	17th March 1910, Saint-Victurnien	Oradour-sur-Glane
67	Boissou (Jeanne)		24th November 1933, Oradour-sur-Glane	Mas-de-l'Arbre, Oradour-sur-Glane
68	Bonnet (Madeleine)	Maid	7th August 1926, orphan in local authority care	Oradour-sur-Glane
69	Bonnet (Marie)		13th Febuary 1934, Oradour-sur-Glane	Les Bordes, Oradour-sur-Glane
70	Bordenave (Jean)	Market trader	7th April 1922, Bordeaux	Oradour-sur-Glane
71	Bossavie (Hélène)		19th May1933, orphan in local authority care	Le Mas-du-Puy, Oradour-sur-Glane
72	Bouchoule (Léopold)	Baker	21st April 1899, Oradour-sur-Glane	Oradour-sur-Glane
73	Bouillère (Odette)	Post master	18th November 1903, Eymoutiers	Oradour-sur-Glane

NUMBER	NAME AND CHRISTIAN NAME	PROFESSION	DATE OF BIRTH	PLACE OF RESIDENCE
74	Bouchoulle (Henri)	Student	6th April 1926, Limoges	Oradour-sur-Glane
75	Bouchoulle (Roger)		23rd November 1929, Oradour-sur-Glane	Oradour-sur-Glane
76	Boulesteix (Claude)		4th December 1937, Oradour-sur-Glane	Oradour-sur-Glane
77	Boulesteix (Christiane)		28th Febuary 1931, Oradour-sur-Glane	Oradour-sur-Glane
78	Mme Pradignac (Anne), née Boulesteix	Farmer	20th October 1877, Vayres	La Malaise, Saint-Brice
79	Boulestin (Marcel)		18th June 1936, Oradour-sur-Glane	Orbagnac, Oradour-sur-Glane
80	Boulestin (Lucien)		18th June 1936, Oradour-sur-Glane	Orbagnac, Oradour-sur-Glane
81	Boutaud (Joseph)	Cobbler	27th May 1912, Saint-Victurnien	Oradour-sur-Glane
82	Boutaud (Marie)		2nd September 1938, Veyrac	Oradour-sur-Glane
83	Brandy (François)	Farmer	21st April 1899, Oradour-sur-Glane	Bellevue, Oradour-sur-Glane
84	Mme Lamaud (Marie), née Brandy		10th December 1897, Oradour-sur-Glane	Bellevue, Oradour-sur-Glane
85	Brandy (Yvonne)	Station master	13th August 1918, Oradour-sur-Glane	Oradour-sur-Glane

No.	Name	Occupation	Date and place of birth	Address
86	Brandy (Antoinette)	Glover	16th May 1923, Oradour-sur-Glane	Oradour-sur-Glane
87	Bricaut (Rolland)		15th October 1935, Limoges	Le Glanet, Oradour-sur-Glane
88	Brissaud (François)	Cobbler	29th May 1871, Oradour-sur-Glane	Oradour-sur-Glane
89	Brissaud (Francine)	Housewife	27th March 1924, Oradour-sur-Glane	Le Vignaud, Oradour-sur-Glane
90	Brissaud (Marcel)	Cartwright	30th September 1892, Veyrac	Le Vignaud, Oradour-sur-Glane
91	Brouillaud (François)	Hairdresser	18th july 1873, Peyrilhac	Oradour-sur-Glane
92	Mme Bergmann (Maria), née Broustein		17th May 1916, Erstein	Oradour-sur-Glane
93	Brouillaud (Jeanne-Marie)	Cleaning woman	27th May1890, Oradour-sur-Glane	Oradour-sur-Glane
94	Brugeron (André)		11th March 1938, Oradour-sur-Glane	Le Repaire, Oradour-sur-Glane
95	Brugeron (René)		29th April 1934, Oradour-sur-Glane	Le Repaire, Oradour-sur-Glane
96	Buisson (Jeanne)		22nd May 1933, Montreuil-sous-Bois	122, rue de Paris, Montreuil-sous-Bois (Seine)
97	Mme Compain (Marie), née Buisson	Baker	22nd October 1904, La Chapelle-Montbrandeix	Oradour-sur-Glane
98	Mme Besson (Marguerite), née Buraud	Unemployed	20th July 1889, Cieux	Oradour-sur-Glane
99	Bureau (Fernand)		11th October 1935, Oradour-sur-Glane	Le Repaire, Oradour-sur-Glane

NUMBER	NAME AND CHRISTIAN NAME	PROFESSION	DATE OF BIRTH	PLACE OF RESIDENCE
100	Canin (Guy)		6th December 1931	Le Repaire, Oradour-sur-Glane
101	Carignon (Jean)		28th June 1935, Paris 15ᵉ	Oradour-sur-Glane
102	Chabert (René)		30th May 1934, Paris 10ᵉ	Oradour-sur-Glane
103	Widow Mᵐᵉ Doire (Marie), née Chaleix	Unemployed	28th April 1872, Javerdat	Oradour-sur-Glane
104	Widow Mᵐᵉ Mirablon (Anna), née Chaleix	Unemployed	12th March1885, Oradour-sur-Glane	14, avenue de Toulouse, Limoges
105	Mᵐᵉ Lesparat (Maria), née Chaleix		22nd Febuary 1888, Oradour-sur-Glane	Oradour-sur-Glane
106	Chapelle (Jean-Baptiste)	Priest	3rd June1873, Nedde	Oradour-sur-Glane
107	Widow Mᵐᵉ Rulière (Marie), née Charton	Unemployed	23rd May 1884, Saint-Victurnien	17, rue du Clos-Sainte-Marie, Limoges
108	Charton (Simone)	Domestic	18th April 1927, Saint-Priest-sous-Aixe	Oradour-sur-Glane
109	Chastang (Jeanne)	Domestic	8th January 1887, Saint-Clément (Corrèze)	Oradour-sur-Glane
110	Chauzat (Camille)		10th August 1937, Oradour-sur-Glane	Lespinas, Oradour-sur-Glane

No.	Name	Occupation	Date and place of birth	Residence
111	Chauzat (Marcelle)	.	25th November 1934, Oradour-sur-Glane	Lespinas, Oradour-sur-Glane
112	Chazeaubeneix (Marie)	Farmer	8th September 1910, Javerdat	La Valette, Javerdat
113	Chénieux (Marie-Amélie)		20th October 1934, Oradour-sur-Glane	Le Repaire, Oradour-sur-Glane
114	Widow Mme Lavérine (Catherine), née Chéroux	Unemployed	14th October 1862, Saint-Victurnien	Oradour-sur-Glane
115	Clavaud (Armand)	Pensionerr	12th june 1862, Oradour-sur-Glane	Oradour-sur-Glane
116	Clavaud (Lucien)		13th Febuary 1926, Oradour-sur-Glane	La Valade, Oradour-sur-Glane
117	Mme Gauteyroux (Eugénie), née Clavaud	Unemployed	11th Febuary 1906, Oradour-sur-Glane	La Plaine, Veyrac
118	Mme Pister (Marie), née Claude		September 1912, Metz	Oradour-sur-Glane
119	Colin (Simone)		3rd March 1936, Limoges	Le Theil, Oradour-sur-Glane
120	Colin (Marcelle)		4th April 1934, Oradour-sur-Glane	Le Theil, Oradour-sur-Glane
121	Colin (Bernard)		14th May 1935, Paris 18e	La Fauvette, Oradour-sur-Glane
122	Compain (Maurice)	Baker	4th June1900, Oradour-sur-Glane	Oradour-sur-Glane
123	Widow Mme Gustin (Berthe), née Coppenolle	Unemployed	4th July 1880, Roubaix	L'Auze, Oradour-sur-Glane

NUMBER	NAME AND CHRISTIAN NAME	PROFESSION	DATE OF BIRTH	PLACE OF RESIDENCE
124	Widow Mme Coldeboeuf (Marie), née Cordeau	Day labourer	15th August1897, Saint-Junien	Oradour-sur-Glane
125	Cordeau (Bernadette)	AApprentie dressmaker	23rd April 1928, Oradour-sur-Glane	Les Bordes, Oradour-sur-Glane
126	Coudert (Pierre)		7th May 1938.	Le Mas-du-Puy, Oradour-sur-Glane
127	Couturier (Ginette)	Typist	13th August 1921, Limoges	20, rue Manigne, Limoges
128	Mme Dupic (Jean), née Couty (Marie)	Unemployed	29th August 1902, Veyrac	Oradour-sur-Glane
129	Mme Leblanc (Hortense), née Couty	Unemployed	4th Jully 1881, Veyrac	Oradour-sur-Glane
130	Couty (Odette)	Teacher	1st May1921, Saint-Sulpice-Laurière	46, rue du Grand-Treuil, Limoges
131	Couvidou (Georgette)		14th September 1934, Veyrac	Le Mas-du-Puy, Oradour-sur-Glane
132	Mme Brassart (Jeanne), née Crombe		17th Febuary 1889, Roubaix	L'Auze, Oradour-sur-Glane
133	Couvidou (Edmond)		3rd June 1937, Veyrac	Le Mas-du-Puy, Oradour-sur-Glane
134	Mme Bichaud (Yvette), née Crouzi	Dressmaker	14th May 1920, Limoges	Rue du Clos-Jargot, Limoges

	Name	Occupation	Date and place of birth	Residence
135	Dagoury (Léonie)	Dressmaker	21st Febuary 1915, Verneuil-sur-Vienne	Oradour-sur-Glane
136	Dagoury (Thérèse)		18th December 1940, Oradour-sur-Glane	Oradour-sur-Glane
137	Debuyser (Georges)		23rd December 1937, Limoges	Laplaud, Oradour-sur-Glane
138	Widow Mᵐᵉ Gélain (Yvonne), née Decanter		17th July 1892, Merris (Nord)	Oradour-sur-Glane
139	Deglane (André)	Farmer	3rd August1870, Javerdat	Champ-du-Bois, Oradour-sur-Glane
140	Deglane (Pierre)	Farmer	13th June 1912, Oradour-sur-Glane	Chez Penot, Oradour-sur-Glane
141	Deglane (René)		15th October 1934, Oradour-sur-Glane	Les Bordes, Oradour-sur-Glane
141a	Mᵐᵉ Deglane (Augustine), née Francillon		15th January 1887, La Croisille (Haute-Vienne)	Oradour-sur-Glane
142	Mᵐᵉ Boutaud (Marie), née Delage	Glover	29th June 1908, Veyrac	Oradour-sur-Glane
143	Delavault (Yvonne)		2nd October 1931.	Oradour-sur-Glane
144	Delhoume (Pierre)	Foreman	10th March 1890, Limoges	1, Cité Casimir-Ranson, Limoges
145	Delhoume (Yvonne)	Transferer on china	27th October 1921, Limoges	1, Cité Casimir-Ranson, Limoges
146	Widow Mᵐᵉ Pinède (Gabrielle), née Delvaille	Unemployed	27th November 1880, Bayonne	Oradour-sur-Glane

NUMBER	NAME AND CHRISTIAN NAME	PROFESSION	DATE OF BIRTH	PLACE OF RESIDENCE
147	Demery (Henri)		1st October 1932, Oradour-sur-Glane	Le Repaire, Oradour-sur-Glane
148	Demery (Marcelle)		10th July 1934, Brigueil	Oradour-sur-Glane
149	Demery (André)		29th January 1931, Oradour-sur-Glane	Bel-Air, Oradour-sur-Glane
150	Demery (Ernest)		2nd April 1933, Oradour-sur-Glane	Oradour-sur-Glane
151	Denis (Léon)	wine merchant	16th Febuary 1884, Oradour-sur-Glane	Oradour-sur-Glane.
152	Mme Texereau (Simone), née Denis	Unemployed	2nd November 1911, Saint-Fiel	Oradour-sur-Glane
153	Depierrefiche (Andrée)	Shop assistant	3rd December 1921, Oradour-sur-Glane	Oradour-sur-Glane
154	Depierrefiche (Jean)	Smith	16th January 1884, Oradour-sur-Glane	Oradour-sur-Glane
155	Desbordes (Jean)	Farmer	3rd September 1898, Oradour-sur-Glane	Chez Magnaud, Oradour-sur-Glane
156	Desbordes (Louis)		3rd October 1932, Oradour-sur-Glane	Chez Magnaud, Oradour-sur-Glane
157	Desbordes (Lucien)	Farmer	20th March 1927, Oradour-sur-Glane	Chez Magnaud, Oradour-sur-Glane

	Name	Occupation	Date and place of birth	Residence
158	Widow Mᵐᵉ Desroches (Marguerite), née Desbordes	Day labourer	70 years old	Chez Magnaud, Oradour-sur-Glane
159	Deschamps (Claudine)		8th August 1931, Oradour-sur-Glane	La Fauvette, Oradour-sur-Glane
160	Deschamps (Renée)		28th December 1833, Oradour-sur-Glane	La Fauvette, Oradour-sur-Glane
161	Deschamps (Huguette)		15th December 1936, Oradour-sur-Glane	La Fauvette, Oradour-sur-Glane
162	Deschamps (Maryse)		21st September 1938, Oradour-sur-Glane	La Fauvette, Oradour-sur-Glane
163	Descubes (Jacques)	Farm hand	29th May 1879, Saint-Junien	Oradour-sur-Glane
164	Mᵐᵉ Faucher (Eugénie), née Descubes	Unemployed	23rd March 1914, Veyrac	Oradour-sur-Glane
165	Denoyer (André)	Chemist's employee	11th March 1929, Paris 6ᵉ	Oradour-sur-Glane
166	Denoyer (Christian)		10th June 1934, Paris 8e	Oradour-sur-Glane
167	Denoyer (Micheline)		2nd November 1935, Paris, 17ᵉ	Oradour-sur-Glane
168	Désourteaux (Etienne)	Townhall secretary	1st January 1910, Oradour-sur-Glane	Oradour-sur-Glane
169	Désourteaux (Paul-Emile)	ShopKeeper	15th January 1905, Oradour-sur-Glane	Oradour-sur-Glane
170	Désourteaux (Jacques)	Doctor	29th December 1905, Oradour-sur-Glane	Oradour-sur-Glane

NUMBER	NAME AND CHRISTIAN NAME	PROFESSION	DATE OF BIRTH	PLACE OF RESIDENCE
171	Désourteaux (Anne-Marie)		28th April 1932, Oradour-sur-Glane	Oradour-sur-Glane
172	Désourteaux (Geneviève)		8th July 1935, Oradour-sur-Glane	Oradour-sur-Glane
173	Desroches (Guy)		20th December 1943, Oradour-sur-Glane	Oradour-sur-Glane
174	Desroches (Georges)		13th August 1941, Oradour-sur-Glane	Oradour-sur-Glane
175	Desroches (Ginette)		28th July 1937, Oradour-sur-Glane	Oradour-sur-Glane
176	Desroches (Monique)		8th August 1935, Oradour-sur-Glane	Oradour-sur-Glane
177	Desseix (Jacques)		8th November 1940, Oradour-sur-Glane	Oradour-sur-Glane
178	Widow Mme Desseix (Marguerite), née Desseix	Farmer	31st October 1879, Veyrac	Bellevue, Oradour-sur-Glane
179	Desvignes (Jean)		1st Febuary 1931, Oradour-sur-Glane	Oradour-sur-Glane
180	Desvignes (Yves)		26th September 1934, Oradour-sur-Glane	Oradour-sur-Glane
181	Desvignes (Odile)		2nd Febuary 1937, Oradour-sur-Glane	Oradour-sur-Glane

No.	Name	Occupation	Date	Place
182	Desvignes (Jean)		24th November 1865	Oradour-sur-Glane
183	Mme Bichaud (Maria), née Deserces	Glover	15th November 1901, Cieux	Oradour-sur-Glane
184	Doire (Jean-Baptiste)	Well-digger	3rd August 1875, Oradour-sur-Glane	Oradour-sur-Glane
185	Doire (Marcelle)	Dressmaker	29th May May 1927, Oradour-sur-Glane	Oradour-sur-Glane
186	Mme Telles (Maria), née Dominguez		15th August 1913, San Feliu de Leobregat (Espagne)	Oradour-sur-Glane
187	Doutre (Martial)	Carpenter	31st May 1893, Chaillac	Oradour-sur-Glane
188	Doutre (Charles)	Carpenter	18th June 1926, Oradour-sur-Glane	Oradour-sur-Glane
189	Widow Mme Ducharlet (Marie), née Ducharlet	Cultivatrice	10th March 1889, Cieux	Oradour-sur-Glane
190	Mme Ducharlet (Marie), née Duchazeaubeneix	Farmer	10th September 1879, Saint-Brice	La Valade, Oradour-sur-Glane
191	Mme Depierrefiche (Marie), née Dufour		14th July 1889, Oradour-sur-Glane	Oradour-sur-Glane
192	Dupic (Pierre)		9th September 1872, Oradour-sur-Glane	La Fauvette, Oradour-sur-Glane
193	Dupic (François)		20th April 1894, Oradour-sur-Glane	Le Vignaud, Oradour-sur-Glane

NUMBER	NAME AND CHRISTIAN NAME	PROFESSION	DATE OF BIRTH	PLACE OF RESIDENCE
194	Dupic (Jean)		26th January 1879, Oradour-sur-Glane	Oradour-sur-Glane.
195	Dupic (Hubert)		12th november 1922, Oradour-sur-Glane	Oradour-sur-Glane
196	Widow Mᵐᵉ Colombier (Anne-Marie), née Duquéroix		18th January 1874, Veyrac	Oradour-sur-Glane
197	Duquéroix (Pierre), dit André	Day labourer	28th November 1897, Oradour-sur-Glane	Oradour-sur-Glane
198	Duquéroix (Angélique)		19th May 1921, Oradour-sur-Glane	Oradour-sur-Glane
199	Mᵐᵉ Senon (Anna), née Durand		6th June 1874, Marcenat (Cantal)	Oradour-sur-Glane
200	Mᵐᵉ Désourteaux (Pierre), née Dutreix (Marie)	Unemployed	15th March 1880, Jussey (Haute-Saône)	Oradour-sur-Glane
201	Duvernet (Adrien)	Farmer	17th December 1924, Cieux	Chez Penot, Oradour-sur-Glane
202	Duvernet (René)	Farmer	8th April 1935, Cieux	Chez Penot, Oradour-sur-Glane
203	Engiel (Raymond)		24th June 1933, Nancy	La-Croix-du-Bois-du-Loup, Oradour-sur-Glane
204	Mᵐᵉ Joachin Gil-Egéa (Francisca), née Espinosa	Unemployed	16th October 1895, Alcaniz (Espagne)	Oradour-sur-Glane

	Name	Occupation	Date and place of birth	Residence
205	Espinosa-Juanos (Carmen)	Domestic	6th September 1914, Barcelone (Espagne)	Oradour-sur-Glane
206	Faucher (Renée)		24th Febuary 1939, Mmagnac-Laval	Oradour-sur-Glane
207	Faugeras (Jean-Claude)		15th January 1935, Limoges	Le Repaire, Oradour-sur-Glane
208	Faure (Aubin)	Unemployed	11th April 1875, Saint-Sulpice-d'Excidueil (Dordogne)	Oradour-sur-Glane
209	Mme Poutaraud (Renée), née Faure	Unemployed	1st September 1912, Ambazac	Oradour-sur-Glane
210	Widow Mme Barthélémy (Emilie), née Folliot	Unemployed	24th December 1868, Paris 10^e	Oradour-sur-Glane
211	Mme Rousseau (Jeanne), née Forest	Teacher	21st January 1896, Rancon	Oradour-sur-Glane
212	Forest (Dominique)		21st October 1937, Saint-Cloud	Laplaud, Oradour-sur-Glane
213	Forest (Michel)		21st May 1924, Guéret	Oradour-sur-Glane
214	Fougeras (Marie), divorcée Fau	Unemployed	3rd October 1884, Oradour-sur-Glane	Oradour-sur-Glane
215	Widow Mme Raynaud (Marguerite), née Foussat		13th August 1853, Javerdat	Oradour-sur-Glane
216	Francillon (Gabriel)	Unemployed	2nd August 1856, La-Croizille-sur-Briance	Oradour-sur-Glane
217	Mme Vevaud (Marie), née Frontout	Farmer	13th February 1907, Oradour-sur-Glane	Le Mas-du-Puy, Oradour-sur-Glane

NUMBER	NAME AND CHRISTIAN NAME	PROFESSION	DATE OF BIRTH	PLACE OF RESIDENCE
218	Widow Mme Redon (Marie), née Fumet	Unemployed	5th July 1873, Nieul	Oradour-sur-Glane
218a	Mme Vignal (Sophie), née Garayt		24th January 1880 Les Ollières (Ardèche)	Oradour-sur-Glane
219	Garaud (André)		19th January 1936, Oradour-sur-Glane	La Fauvette, Oradour-sur-Glane
220	Widow Mme Ribière (Marceline), née Garaud	Unemployed	10th Ocober 1903, Saint-Junien	31, Faubourg du Pont-Neuf, Limoges
221	Widow Mme Mosnier (Marguerite), née Garaud	Unemployed	26th March 1887, Oradour-sur-Glane	Oradour-sur-Glane
222	Garaud (Martial), dit Marcelin	Bricklayer	6th January 1880, Oradour-sur-Glane	Les Bordes, Oradour-sur-Glane
223	Mme Canitrot (Marie-Louise), née Garrigues	Retired teacher	5th May 1890, Narbonne	8, Boulevard Louis-Blanc, Montpellier
224	Mme Denoyer (Anna), née Gauduffe	Unemployed	12th November 1906, Oradour-sur-Glane	Oradour-sur-Glane
225	Gaudy (Léonard)	Day labourer	70 years old	Oradour-sur-Glane
226	Mme Pasquet (Marie), née Gaudy	Farmer	12th August 1898, Cieux	Bellevue, Javerdat
227	Gaudy (Marcelle)		29th October 1932, Peyrilhac	Laplaud, Oradour-sur-Glane

	Name	Occupation	Date of birth	Address
228	Gaudy (Roger)		10th November 1930, Oradour-sur-Glane	Laplaud, Oradour-sur-Glane
229	Gaudy (Maurice)		7th July 1936, Peyrilhac	Oradour-sur-Glane
230	Gaudy (Pierre)		7th May 1934, Oradour-sur-Glane	Theineix, Oradour-sur-Glane
231	Gazan (Roger)	Domestic	18th July 1927e	Bellevue, Oradour-sur-Glane
232	Mme Bardet (Yvonne), née Gendraud	Glover	22nd April1913, Cieux	Villa "André", Oradour-sur-Glane
233	Gelain (Bernard)		9th January 1928, Saint-Pol-sur-Mer (Nord)	Oradour-sur-Glane
234	Gelain (Marie-louise)		18th December 1923, Saint-Pol-sur-Mer (Nord)	Oradour-sur-Glane
235	Mme Darthout (Louise-Yvonne), née Georges		11th April 1918, Javerdat	Oradour-sur-Glane
236	Georges (Hélène)	Farmer	8th April 1924, Cieux	Orbagnac, Oradour-sur-Glane
237	Giachino (Auguste)	Turner-Mechanic	30th April 1898, Nice	14, avenue Bornala, Nice
238	Mme Binet (Andrée), née Gibaud	TTeacher	5th March 1914, Nexon	Oradour-sur-Glane
239	Gil Espinoza (Pilar)		5th September 1929, Alcaniz (Espagne)	Oradour-sur-Glane
240	Gil Espinoza (Francisca)		5th September 1929, Alcaniz (Espagne)	Oradour-sur-Glane

NUMBER	NAME AND CHRISTIAN NAME	PROFESSION	DATE OF BIRTH	PLACE OF RESIDENCE
241	Mᵐᵉ Sansonnet (Marguerite), née Giraud	Unemployed	20th July 1877, Saint-Yriex	La Malaise, Saint-Brice
242	Girard (Charles)	Farmer	3rd September 1902, Charly	Oradour-sur-Glane
243	Girard (Yvette)		4th May 1935, Metz	Oradour-sur-Glane
244	Girard (Jeannie)		7th April 1937, Metz	Oradour-sur-Glane
245	Girard (Constant)	Farmer	5th April 1873, Charly	Oradour-sur-Glane
246	Giroux (Pierre)		29th November 1867, Oradour-sur-Glane	Le Vignaud, Oradour-sur-Glane
247	Mᵐᵉ Joyeux (Marie-Louise), née Giroux	Glover	19th June 1908, Oradour-sur-Glane	Le Vignaud, Oradour-sur-Glane
248	Godfrin (Arthur)	Assistant-baker	20th January 1907, Charly	Oradour-sur-Glane
249	Godfrin (Josette)		18th May 1941, Saint-Junien	Oradour-sur-Glane
250	Godfrin (Marie-Jeanne)		27th September 1931, Charly	Oradour-sur-Glane
251	Godfrin (Claude)		14th Febuary 1940, Metz	Oradour-sur-Glane
252	Godfrin (Pierrette)		18th May 1933, Charly	Oradour-sur-Glane
253	Mᵐᵉ Kauzler (Maria), née Goldmann	Unemployed	16th April 1899, Warschau (Pologne)	Oradour-sur-Glane

	Name	Occupation	Date/Place of birth	Residence
254	Gougeon (Fernand)	Teacher	11th May 1911, Metz	Oradour-sur-Glane
255	Gougeon (Gérard)		5 years old	Oradour-sur-Glane
256	Gougeon (Claude)		4 years old	Oradour-sur-Glane
257	Gourceau (Andrée)		23rd October 1934, Oradour-sur-Glane	Rentier, Oradour-sur-Glane
258	Mme Senon (Louise), née Gourceau	Unemployed	1893	Oradour-sur-Glane
259	Mme Milord (Mélanie), née Gourinat	Inn Keeper	11th January1890, Oradour-sur-Glane	Oradour-sur-Glane
260	Mme Lesparat (Marcelle), née Grand	Dress maker	9th June 1912, Veyrac	Oradour-sur-Glane
261	Granet (Aline)		25th January 1937, Peyrilhac	Valeix, Oradour-sur-Glane
262	Widow Mme Garrigues (Marie), née Guérineau	Unemployed	26th October 1856, Poitiers	8, boulevard Louis-Blanc, Montpellier
263	Guiomnet (Jacqueline)		12th September 1934, Paris 18^e	Boulevard Saint-Michel, Paris, 5^e
264	Gaillot (Hubert)		12th May 1939, Metz	La Basse-Forêt, Oradour-sur-Glane
265	Gaillot (Daniel)		24th August 1941, Saint-Junien	La Basse-Forêt, Oradour-sur-Glane
266	Haas (René)		8th December1940, Oradour-sur-Glane	Oradour-sur-Glane
267	Haas (Huguette)		13th January 1938, Metz	Oradour-sur-Glane

NUMBER	NAME AND CHRISTIAN NAME	PROFESSION	DATE OF BIRTH	PLACE OF RESIDENCE
268	Haas (Jules-Alphonse)		9th December 1911, Remering-Lès-Hargaten	Oradour-sur-Glane
269	Haas (Jules-Paul)		15th April 1944, Oradour-sur-Glane	Oradour-sur-Glane
270	Hébras (Denise)		20th Febuary 1935, Oradour-sur-Glane	Oradour-sur-Glane
271	Hebras (Georgette)	Nurse	20th January1922, Buissière-Poitevine	Oradour-sur-Glane
272	Henry (Michelle)		20th January 1942, Sartrouville	1, rue de Verdun, Sartrouville
273	Widow Mme Pister (Mélanie), née Hennequin	Unemployed	3rd April 1880, Flevy	Oradour-sur-Glane
274	Hyvernaud (Marcel)		16th July 1931, Oradour-sur-Glane	Le Breuil, Oradour-sur-Glane
275	Hyvernaud (André)		21st June 1937, Verneuil-sur-Vienne	Oradour-sur-Glane
276	Hyvernaud (René)		20th July 1933, Oradour-sur-Glane	Mazenty, Oradour-sur-Glane
277	Hyvernaud (Fernand)	Unemployed	17th October 1898, Limoges	Oradour-sur-Glane
278	Hyvernaud (Albert)	Farmerr	22nd July 1828, Oradour-sur-Glane	Oradour-sur-Glane

No.	Name	Occupation	Date and place of birth	Residence
279	Hyvernaud (Raymonde)		24th June 1932, Oradour-sur-Glane	Oradour-sur-Glane
280	Hyvernaud (Yvonne)		3rd December 1935, Oradour-sur-Glane	Oradour-sur-Glane
281	Hyvernaud (Gabriel)		6th June 1938, Oradour-sur-Glane	Oradour-sur-Glane
282	Hyvernaud (Roland)		11th November 1939, Oradour-sur-Glane	Oradour-sur-Glane
283	Hyvernaud (André)		15th December 1940, Oradour-sur-Glane	Oradour-sur-Glane
284	Ito (Jean)	Chimney sweeper	22nd January 1899, Saint-Junien	Oradour-sur-Glane
285	Jouhaud (Raymond)	Packer	30th July 1908, Limoges	22, cité Beaublanc, Limoges
286	Joyeux (Henri)		6th Febuary1939, Oradour-sur-Glane	Le Vignaud, Oradour-sur-Glane
287	Joyeux (Roger)		15th March 1940, Oradour-sur-Glane	Le Vignaud, Oradour-sur-Glane
288	Joyeux (Marcel)	Mechanic	30th March 1921, Limoges	Soudanas, Panazol
289	Mme Mondot (Léonie), née Joyeux	Unemployed	5th December1889, Oradour-sur-Glane	Oradour-sur-Glane
290	Mme Bardet (Marie-Louise), née Jude	Unemployed	7th January 1911, Saint-Junien	Oradour-sur-Glane
291	Juge (Pierre)	Farmer	14th May1911, Oradour-sur-Glane	Les Brégères, Oradour-sur-Glane
292	Juge (Anne-Marie)		29th November 1941, Oradour-sur-Glane	Oradour-sur-Glane

NUMBER	NAME AND CHRISTIAN NAME	PROFESSION	DATE OF BIRTH	PLACE OF RESIDENCE
293	Juge (Jean-Pierre)		25th March 1937, Oradour-sur-Glane	Les Brégères, Oradour-sur-Glane
294	Juge (Gilbert)	Farmer	3rd May 1879, Oradour-sur-Glane	Les Brégères, Oradour-sur-Glane
295	Kanzler (Joseph)	Hairdresser	11th October 1893, Budapest	Oradour-sur-Glane
296	Kanzler (Dora)		14th January 1930, Strasbourg	Oradour-sur-Glane
297	Kanzler (Simone)		12th July 1934, Strasbourg	Oradour-sur-Glane
298	Mme Girard (Clotilde), née Koppe	Unemployed	30th May 1907, Burtoncourt (Moselle)	Oradour-sur-Glane
299	Labarde (Pierre)	Farmer	22nd June 1879, Peyrilhac	La Boine, Veyrac
300	Widow Mme Desbordes (Jeanne), née Lacroix	Farmer	5th August 1874, Oradour-sur-Glane	Oradour-sur-Glane
301	Lacroix (Jean)		25th June 1941, Oradour-sur-Glane	Puy-Gaillard, Oradour-sur-Glane
302	Lacroix (Monique)		22nd April 1943, Oradour-sur-Glane	Oradour-sur-Glane
303	Lacroix (Roland)		29th May 1944, Oradour-sur-Glane	Oradour-sur-Glane
304	Ladegaillerie (Françoise)	Cleaning woman	5th January 1877, Blond	Oradour-sur-Glane

305	Mᵐᵉ Lalue (Marie), née Lafont	Farmer	16th September 1877, Saulgond	Oradour-sur-Glane
306	Widow Mᵐᵉ Petit (Anne), née Lagrogerie	Unemployed	20th November 1887, Oradour-sur-Glane	Oradour-sur-Glane
307	Laine (Gisèle)		9th March 1942, Nonvilliers-Grandhoux (Eure-et-Loire)	Oradour-sur-Glane
308	Lalue (Léonard)	Faarmer Bricklayer	8th October 1873, Peyrilhac	Oradour-sur-Glane
309	Lamarche (Jean)	Day labourer	5th August 1874, Peyrilhac	Oradour-sur-Glane
310	Lamaud (Jean)	Farmer	19th September 1897, Oradour-sur-Glane	Bellevue, Oradour-sur-Glane
311	Mᵐᵉ Darthout (Anna), née Lamaud	Unemployed	24th October 1904, Saint-Cyr	Oradour-sur-Glane
312	Lamaud (François)	Farmer	29th August 1872, Oradour-sur-Glane	Bellevue, Oradour-sur-Glane
313	Lamaud (Marie-Thérèse)		16th May 1940, Oradour-sur-Glane	Bellevue, Oradour-sur-Glane
314	Lamige (Arsène)	Baker	12th January 1929, Oradour-sur-Glane	Chez Lanie, Oradour-sur-Glane
315	Lamige (Germaine)		27th Febuary 1938, Oradour-sur-Glane	Oradour-sur-Glane
316	Lamige (Marcel)		27th Febuary 1937, Oradour-sur-Glane	Oradour-sur-Glane

NUMBER	NAME AND CHRISTIAN NAME	PROFESSION	DATE OF BIRTH	PLACE OF RESIDENCE
317	Lanot (Jeanne)		10th June 1937, Oradour-sur-Glane	Oradour-sur-Glane
318	Lanot (Anne-Marie)		20th July 1932, Oradour-sur-Glane	Oradour-sur-Glane
319	Mme Barataud (Marguerite), née Laplaud		10th June 1876, Nieul	Les Bordes, Oradour-sur-Glane
320	Mme Avril (Adrienne-Odette), née Laroudie	Unemployed	10th March 1914, Nieul	Oradour-sur-Glane
321	Widow Mme Vergnaud (Françoise), née Lasséchère	Unemployed	23rd May 1872, Cieux	Oradour-sur-Glane
322	Mme Texier (Marie), née Lathière	Unemployed	16th November 1914, Saint-Brice	La Malaise, Saint-Brice
323	Lavaud (André-Jean)		15th October 1931, Oradour-sur-Glane	La Tuilière-des-Bordes, Oradour-sur-Glane
324	Lavergne (Antoine)	Farmer	3rd September 1904, Cieux	Theineix, Oradour-sur-Glane
325	Lavergne (Gilbert)		26th September 1930, Cieux	Oradour-sur-Glane
326	Lavergne (Jean)		19th December 1879, Blond	Oradour-sur-Glane
327	de Laverine (Léon-Hubert)	Unemployed	6th May 1900, Soissons	Chalet "Saint-Vincent", Oradour-sur-Glane
328	de Laverine (Mireille)	Unemployed	31st January 1925, Oradour-sur-Glane	Chalet "Saint-Vincent", Oradour-sur-Glane

#	Name	Occupation	Date/Place of Birth	Residence
329	de Laverine (Thérèse)	Unemployed	6th August 1926, Oradour-sur-Glane	Chalet "Saint-Vincent", Oradour-sur-Glane
330	Widow Mme Avril (Marie), née Laverine	InnKeeperr	1st August 1879, Oradour-sur-Glane	Oradour-sur-Glane
331	Mme Doutre (Catherine), née Laverine	Unemployed	23rd April 1891, Oradour-sur-Glane	Oradour-sur-Glane
332	Lavisse (Jean-Robert)		23rd September 1931, Paris 15^e	Oradour-sur-Glane
333	Laurence (Henri)	Retired policeman	21st September 1889, Catelier (Seine-Inférieure)	Oradour-sur-Glane
334	Laurence (Bernard)		2nd December 1934, Paris 4^e	Oradour-sur-Glane
335	Laurence (Geneviève)		10th May 1937, Paris 4^e	Oradour-sur-Glane
336	Leblanc (Jules)	Mill owner	25th November 1875, Benayes (Corrèze)	Oradour-sur-Glane
337	Lebraud (Emma)	Dressmaker	16th August 1925, Cieux	Charrat, Cieux
338	Widow Mme Bélivier (Anne), née Lecompte	Farmer	13th May 1826, Cognac-le-Froid	Les Bregêres, Oradour-sur-Glane
339	Lamarche (Catherine), née Ledot	Unemployed	69 years old, Cieux	Oradour-sur-Glane
340	Ledot (Martial)	Farmer	4th July 1881, Cieux	Le Repaire, Oradour-sur-Glane
341	Mme Bélivier (Angèle), née Léger	Farmer	17th January 1901, Oradour-sur-Glane	Les Bregêres, Oradour-sur-Glane
342	Léger (Marcellin)	Farmer	8th August 1879, Oradour-sur-Glane	Le Moulin, Oradour-sur-Glane

NUMBER	NAME AND CHRISTIAN NAME	PROFESSION	DATE OF BIRTH	PLACE OF RESIDENCE
343	Mme Santabien (Madeleine), née Legros	Unemployed	3rd Febuary 1886, Reims	Oradour-sur-Glane
344	Legros (Pierre)		13th Febuary 1923, Coblence (Allemagne)	93, rue du Barbatre, Reims
345	Mme Girard (Marie), née Leid	Farmer	27th April 1876, Sainte-Barbe (Moselle)	Oradour-sur-Glane
346	Lesparat (Jean)	Cartwright	17th January 1881, Cieux	Oradour-sur-Glane
347	Lesparat (Fernand)	Cartwright	9th Febuary 1909, Oradour-sur-Glane	Oradour-sur-Glane
348	Lesparat (Monique)		2nd August1933, Oradour-sur-Glane	Oradour-sur-Glane
349	Mme Ratier (Marie), née Lévèque	Farmer	22nd September 1917, Saint-Laurent-sur-Gorre	Orbagnac, Oradour-sur-Glane
350	Lévèque (Marie-Yvonne)	Farmer	18th May 1924, Limoges	Oradour-sur-Glane
351	Lévignac (Jean-Serge)		5th may 1928, Bergerac	7, chemin des Deux-Routes, Avignon
352	Lévignac (Charles)		29th July 1932, Colmar	7, chemin des Deux-Routes, Avignon
353	Lorente-Pardo (Nouria)		28th September 1935, Barcelone (Espagne)	Oradour-sur-Glane

354	Lorich (Angélique)	Unemployed	27th September 1912, Hottviller (Moselle)	Oradour-sur-Glane
355	Lorich (Jacques)	Priest	25th July 1897, Hottviller (Moselle)	Oradour-sur-Glane
356	Mme Gougeon (Marie), née Lorrain	Unemployed	September 1913, Charly (Moselle)	Oradour-sur-Glane
357	Lorrain (Emile)	Unemployed	15th January 1886, Vigy (Moselle)	Oradour-sur-Glane
358	Lorrain (Paulette)		27th April 1916, Charly (Moselle)	Oradour-sur-Glane
359	Mme Aliotti (Cléa), née Lusina	Unemployed	28th October 1921, Abazzia (Italie)	Oradour-sur-Glane
360	Machefer (Yvette)		18th May 1933, Oradour-sur-Glane	Oradour-sur-Glane
361	Machefer (Désiré)		28th January 1943, Oradour-sur-Glane	Oradour-sur-Glane
362	Machenaud (André)	Dealer	10th October 1883, Chatellerault	Oradour-sur-Glane
363	Machenaud (Denise)	Unemployed	10th October 1922, Paris 15e	Oradour-sur-Glane
364	Mme Godfrin (Georgette), née Maillard	Unemployed	17th April 1909, Argancy (Moselle)	Oradour-sur-Glane
365	Maingraud (Marius)	Unemployed	3rd December 1890, La Rochelle	Oradour-sur-Glane
366	Maire (Gabriel)	Butcher	28th May 1909, Chenières (mmeurthe-et-Moselle)	Oradour-sur-Glane

NUMBER	NAME AND CHRISTIAN NAME	PROFESSION	DATE OF BIRTH	PLACE OF RESIDENCE
367	Widow Mᵐᵉ Boullière (Marie), née Martinet	Unemployed	31st July1872, Eymoutiers	Oradour-sur-Glane
368	Martial (Xavier)		3rd December 1932, Oradour-sur-Glane	Oradour-sur-Glane
369	Widow Mᵐᵉ C. Joyeux (Catherine), née Masmaud	Unemployed	1885	Oradour-sur-Glane
370	Masachs (Emilia)		9th Febuary 1933, Sabadell (Espagne)	La Fauvette, Oradour-sur-Glane
371	Masachs (Angélina)		22nd August 1936, Sabadell (Espagne)	La Fauvette, Oradour-sur-Glane
372	Mathieu (Léon)	Day labourer	5th October1896, Charly (Moselle)	Oradour-sur-Glane
373	Mathieu (Marguerite)	Unemployed	8th September 1899, Charly (Moselle)	Oradour-sur-Glane
374	Mᵐᵉ J. B. Beaulieu (Elisa), née Mauveroux	Unemployed	28th March 1894, Oradour-sur-Glane	Oradour-sur-Glane
375	Mauveroux (Martial)	Unemployed	15th Febuary 1863, Saint-Yriex-sous-Aixe	Oradour-sur-Glane
376	Beaudet (Marie), née Mélier	Glover	9th November 1896, Saint-Brice	Le Vignaud, Oradour-sur-Glane

No.	Name	Occupation	Date and place of birth	Residence
377	Widow Mme Dagoury (Mélanie), née Mélier	InnKeeper	7th January 1895, Saot-Brice	Le Vignaud, Oradour-sur-Glane
378	Mme Bardet (Marie-Claire), née Melledent	Unemployed	28th May 1888, Limoges	Oradour-sur-Glane
379	Widow Mme Brandy (Eugénie), née Mercier	Coffee house keeper	31st December 1894, Oradour-sur-Glane	Oradour-sur-Glane
380	Mercier (René)	Shop keeper	16th April1916, Saint-Victurenien	Oradour-sur-Glane
381	Mercier (Denis)	Farmer	3rd May1890, Oradour-sur-Glane	Puy-Gaillard, Oradour-sur-Glane
382	Mercier (Yvonne)	Farmer	22nd June 1923, Oradour-sur-Glane	Puy-Gaillard, Oradour-sur-Glane
383	Mercier (François)	Farmer	June1861, Saint-Jouvent	Puy-Gaillard, Oradour-sur-Glane
384	Mercier (Mathieu)	Retired Postmaster	13th December 1886, Oradour-sur-Glane	Oradour-sur-Glane
385	Mercier (Marie)	Glover	1st August 1907, Oradour-sur-Glane	Puy-Gaillard, Oradour-sur-Glane
386	Widow Mme Thomas (Marie), née Mérigot	Farmer	30th March 1888, Javerdat	Le Mas-du-Puy, Oradour-sur-Glane
387	Mme Hébras (Marie), née Mérigout	Unemployed	3rd March 1893, Saint-Bonnet-de-Bellac	Oradour-sur-Glane
388	Mme Guyonnet (Marie), née Metche	Domestic	24th August 1886, Buzet-sur-Tarn (Haute-Garonne)	Oradour-sur-Glane
389	Mme Pallier (Françoise), née Metzger	Unemployed	7th July 1909, Besançon	Paris 17e, 11, rue Guillaume-Tell
390	Mme J. Descubes (Marie), née Michelet	Unemployed	27th March 1877, Saint-Gence	Oradour-sur-Glane

NUMBER	NAME AND CHRISTIAN NAME	PROFESSION	DATE OF BIRTH	PLACE OF RESIDENCE
391	Milord (Léon)	InnKeeper	20th Febuary1882, Oradour-sur-Glane	Oradour-sur-Glane
392	Milord (Victor)	Cook	13th July 1914, Oradour-sur-Glane	Limoges, 77, Faubourg Montjovis
393	Milord (Nicolle)		4th December 1939, Saint-Brice	Limoges, 77, Faubourg Montjovis
394	Milord (Marie)		30th January 1944, Limoges	Limoges, 77, Faubourg Montjovis
395	Milord (Robert-François)		19th june, Lyon	Oradour-sur-Glane
396	Vignal			Les Brandes, Oradour-sur-Glane
397	Miozzo (Bruno)	Farmer	29th October 1925, San-Georgio (Italie)	Les Brandes, Oradour-sur-Glane
398	Miozzo (Angèle)	Farmer	10th january1929, Lestreps (Charente)	Les Brandes, Oradour-sur-Glane
399	Miozzo (Armand)	Farmer	8th Febuary 1930, Lesterps (Charente)	Les Brandes, Oradour-sur-Glane
400	Miozzo (Louis)	Farmer	1st Febuary 1932, Lesterps (Charente)	Les Brandes, Oradour-sur-Glane
401	Miozzo (Anna)	Farmer	29th March 1933, Lesterps (Charente)	Les Brandes, Oradour-sur-Glane

	Name	Occupation	Date and place of birth	Address
402	Miozzo (Marcel)	Farmer	22nd October 1934, Excideuil (Charente)	Les Brandes, Oradour-sur-Glane
402 bis	Montazeaud (Pierre)	Notary	21st January 1894, Cieux (Haute-Vienne)	Oradour-sur-Glane
403	Miozzo (Jean)		11th October 1940, Saint-Junien	Les Brandes, Oradour-sur-Glane
404	Mondot (Léonard)	Day labourer	28th August 1887, Périlhac	Oradour-sur-Glane
405	Montazeaud (Antoine)	Disabled veteran 1914-18	14th november 1892, Cieux	20, rue Firmin-Delage, Limoges
406	Mᵐᵉ Pascaud (Denise), née Moreau	Unemployed	13th November 1911, Saint-Marcel (Indre)	Oradour-sur-Glane
407	Moreau (Robert)		21st November 1938, Saint-Junien	Le Mas-du-Puy, Oradour-sur-Glane
408	Moreau (Roger)		6th December 1934, Périlhac	Les Bordes, Oradour-sur-Glane
409	Moreau (Lucie)	Housemaid	16th April 1926, Pupille de l'Assistance publique	Bellevue, Oradour-sur-Glane,
410	Moreau (Pierre)	Bricklayer	10th Febuary 1877, Oradour-sur-Glane	Oradour-sur-Glane
411	Mᵐᵉ Texier (Marie-Louise), née Moreau	Unemployed	20th January 1914, Limoges	Oradour-sur-Glane
412	Widow Mᵐᵉ Senon (Marie), née Morliéras	Unemployed	9th April 1864, Oradour-sur-Glane	Villa André, Oradour-sur-Glane
413	Morliéras (Irène)	Unemployed	15th May 1927, Oradour-sur-Glane	Oradour-sur-Glane

NUMBER	NAME AND CHRISTIAN NAME	PROFESSION	DATE OF BIRTH	PLACE OF RESIDENCE
414	Mme Maingraud (Marie), née Négrot	Unemployed	9th December 1895, Javerdat	Oradour-sur-Glane
415	Neumeyer (Emile-François)	Seminarist	5th January 1923, Schiltigheim (Bas-Rhin)	Oradour-sur-Glane
416	Neumeyer (Odile)	Housemaid	20th August 1911, Strasbourg	Oradour-sur-Glane
417	Nicolas (Jeanne)		6th Febuary 1934, Oradour-sur-Glane	Oradour-sur-Glane
418	Mme Lanot (Marguerite), née Nicolas	Butcher	26th january 1911, Oradour-sur-Glane	Oradour-sur-Glane
419	Mme Brissaud (Catherine), née Nicolas	Unemployed	15th April 1876, Périlhac	Oradour-sur-Glane
420	Mme Thomas (Anne), née Devoyon	Unemployed	70 years old	Oradour-sur-Glane
421	Mme Louis Bardet (Marie), née Normand	Unemployed	13th December 1899, Blond (Haute-Vienne)	Oradour-sur-Glane
422	Pallier (Yves)		13th October 1838, Boulogne-Billancourt (Seine)	11, rue Guillaume-Tell, Paris 17^e
423	Pallier (Huguette)		1st April 1936, Boulogne-Billancourt (Seine)	Oradour-sur-Glane
424	Mme Serrano (Maria), née Pardo	Unemployed	12th December 1913, Murcia (Espagne)	Oradour-sur-Glane

	Name	Occupation	Birth	Residence
425	Mᵐᵉ Laurente (Antonia), née Pardo	Unemployed	4th April 1915, Murcia (Espagne)	Oradour-sur-Glane
426	Pascaud (Marcel)	Chemist	28th July 1912, Chasseneuil (Charente)	Oradour-sur-Glane
427	Pascaud (Jean-Louis)		19th August 1941, Oradour-sur-Glane	Oradour-sur-Glane
428	Mᵐᵉ de Laverine (Antoinette), née Pate	Unemployed	1st September1898, Saint-Rémy (Saône et Loire)	Chalet "Saint-Vincent", Oradour-sur-Glane
429	Penot (Robert)		10th September 1931, Pupille de l'Assistance publique	Bellevue, Oradour-sur-Glane
430	Mᵐᵉ Henry (Gilberte), née Biver	Unemployed	21st June1921, Hayange (Moselle)	1, rue de Verdun, Sartrouville, (Seine-et-Oise)
431	Pérette (Louis)	Unemployed	29th August 1886, Charly (Moselle)	Oradour-sur-Glane
432	Mᵐᵉ Pérette (Lucie), née Holot		25th May 1890, Vigny	Oradour-sur-Glane
433	Mᵐᵉ Sirieix (Elisabeth), née Périgord	Unemployed	19th November 1872, Oradour-sur-Glane	Oradour-sur-Glane
434	Widow Mᵐᵉ Gauduffe (Marguerite), née Petit	Unemployed	27th September 1863, Oradour-sur-Glane	Oradour-sur-Glane
435	Petit (Marcelle)	Hairdresser	9th December 1918, Oradour-sur-Glane	Oradour-sur-Glane

NUMBER	NAME AND CHRISTIAN NAME	PROFESSION	DATE OF BIRTH	PLACE OF RESIDENCE
436	Peyroux (Guy)		11th November 1943, Oradour-sur-Glane	Chez Gaudy, Oradour-sur-Glane
437	Picat (Germaine)		19th September 1930	Orbagnac, Oradour-sur-Glane
438	Picat (Maurice)	Businessman	4th June 1883, Limoges	Oradour-sur-Glane
439	Vergnaud (Maria). Servante de M. Picat		40 years old	Oradour-sur-Glane
440	Mme L. Bouchoulle (Gabrielle), née Pidance	Baker	26th May 1906, Paris 15e	Oradour-sur-Glane
441	Pister (Lucette)		21st January 1942, Oradour-sur-Glane	Oradour-sur-Glane
442	Mme Haas (Marie-Louise), née Pister	Unemployed	15th August 1916, Charly (Moselle)	Oradour-sur-Glane
443	Pister (Auguste)	Cartwright	9th December 1873, Charly (Moselle)	Oradour-sur-Glane
444	Mme Duquéroix (Marie-Louise), née Pommier	Unemployed	14th September 1902, Oradour-sur-Glane	Oradour-sur-Glane
445	Poutaraud (Danielle)		October 1942, Oradour-sur-Glane	Oradour-sur-Glane
446	Poutaraud (Odette)		October 1940, Oradour-sur-Glane	Oradour-sur-Glane

No.	Name	Occupation	Date and place of birth	Residence
447	Poutaraud (Yvette)		7th june 1937, Oradour-sur-Glane	Oradour-sur-Glane
448	Poutaraud (Suzanne)		9th Febuary 1935, Oradour-sur-Glane	Oradour-sur-Glane
449	Poutaraud (Marcel)		18th march 1934, Oradour-sur-Glane	Oradour-sur-Glane
450	Poutaraud (Andrée)		9th Febuary 1933, Ambazac	Oradour-sur-Glane
451	Mᵐᵉ A. Villatte (Christiane), née Praline	Unemployed	20th Febuary 1924, Paris 9ᵉ	12, rue du Docteur-Bergognié, Limoges
452	Mᵐᵉ A. Gibaud (Louise), née Ragot	Unemployed	5th january 1889-, La Meyze	84, Faubourg d'Angoulême, Limoges
453	Rainier (François)	China painter	16th September 1910, Limoges	Maison Gubt, rue Saint-Gence, Limoges,
454	Ramber (Josiane)		16th September 1939, Oradour-sur-Glane	Oradour-sur-Glane
455	Ramnoux (Claude)		4th April 1938, Oradour-sur-Glane	Les Bordes, Oradour-sur-Glane
456	Ramnoux (Jean)	Clog maker	6th May 1904, Oradour-sur-Glane	Oradour-sur-Glane
457	Widow Mᵐᵉ Senon (Françoise), née Ramnoux	Farmer	74 years old	Puy-Gaillard, Oradour-sur-Glane
458	Ratier (Anne-Marie)		7th September 1938, Oradour-sur-Glane	Orbagnac, Oradour-sur-Glane
459	Raynaud (Edith)		9th December 1935, Javerdat	La Valade, Oradour-sur-Glane

NUMBER	NAME AND CHRISTIAN NAME	PROFESSION	DATE OF BIRTH	PLACE OF RESIDENCE
460	Raynaud (Lucien)	Baker	27th March 1913, Couzeix	Oradour-sur-Glane
461	Raynaud (Bernard)		24th March 1941, Oradour-sur-Glane	Oradour-sur-Glane
462	Raynaud (Irène)		6th March 1937, Javerdat	Oradour-sur-Glane
463	Mᵐᵉ Valentin (Marie), née Raynaud	Unemployed	23rd June 1893, Oradour-sur-Glane	Oradour-sur-Glane
464	Mᵐᵉ Pierre Moreau (Marguerite), née Raynaud	Unemployed	24th June 1877, Oradour-sur-Glane	Oradour-sur-Glane
465	Redon (Irène)	Shopkeeper	13th January 1925, Oradour-sur-Glane	Oradour-sur-Glane
466	Widow Mᵐᵉ Lavaud (Louise), née Redon	Unemployed	23rd Novembre 1900, Oradour-sur-Glane	Oradour-sur-Glane
467	Renaud (Annie)		24th April 1940, Oradour-sur-Glane	Oradour-sur-Glane
468	Renaudin (Jules)	Blacksmith	3rd May 1902, Montoy-Flanville (Moselle)	Oradour-sur-Glane
469	Renaudin (Bernadette)		16th May 1937, Metz	Laplaud, Oradour-sur-Glane
470	Restoueix (Hubert)		20th November 1934, Oradour-sur-Glane	Le Repaire, Oradour-sur-Glane

	Name	Occupation	Date and place of birth	Residence
471	Richard (Christian)		28th April 1931, Limoges	La Valade, Oradour-sur-Glane
472	Richard (Jean-Claude)		21st January 1937, Limoges	La Valade, Oradour-sur-Glane
473	Richard (André)	Notary's clerk	13th April 1916, Verrières (Vienne)	20, rue Firmin-Delage, Limoges
474	Roby (Pierre-Maurice)		22nd January 1923, Oradour-sur-Glane	Le Repaire, Oradour-sur-Glane
475	Roby (Marcelle)		1st March 1938, Oradour-sur-Glane	Le Repaire, Oradour-sur-Glane
476	Widow Mme Delpech (Catherine), née Roby	Unemployed	13th September 1864, Oradour-sur-Glane	Oradour-sur-Glane
477	Mme Peyroux (Amélie), née Rouffanche	Farmer	6th May 1923, Saint-Gence	Chez Gaudy, Oradour-sur-Glane
478	Rouffanche (Jean)	Farmer	24th June 1921, Saint-Gence	Chez Gaudy, Oradour-sur-Glane
479	Rouffanche (Andrée)	Farmer	2nd April 1926, Verneuil-sur-Vienne	Chez Gaudy, Oradour-sur-Glane
480	Rouffanche (Simon)	Farmer	29th January 1891, Oradour-sur-Glane	Chez Gaudy, Oradour-sur-Glane
481	Widow Mme Senon (Marguerite), née Rouffanche	Farmer	8th December 1864, Oradour-sur-Glane	Oradour-sur-Glane
482	Roumy (Albert)	Student	17th July 1921, Oradour-sur-Glane	Oradour-sur-Glane
483	Rousseau (Léonard)	Teacher	23rd Febuary 1895, Saint-Denis-des-Murs	Oradour-sur-Glane

NUMBER	NAME AND CHRISTIAN NAME	PROFESSION	DATE OF BIRTH	PLACE OF RESIDENCE
484	Rousseau (Marguerite)	Student	25th November 1923, Vaulry	Oradour-sur-Glane
485	Rousseau (Pierre)		8th March 1928, Vaulry	Oradour-sur-Glane
486	Roussy (Michel)		22nd September 1938, Oradour-sur-Glane	Les Cros, Oradour-sur-Glane
487	Mme J. Lacroix (Olga), née Roussy	Farmer	17th November 1920, Oradour-sur-Glane	Puy Gaillard, Oradour-sur-Glane
488	Mme Thomas (Lucienne), née Ruven	Farmer	15th May1918, Cornoët (Côtes-du-Nord)	Le Mas-du-Puy, Oradour-sur-Glane
489	Mme B. Desvignes (Madeleine), née Sadry	Butcher	19th August 1907, Limoges	Oradour-sur-Glane
490	Sadry (Andrée)	Domestic	19th October1929, Saint-Martin-de-Jussac	Oradour-sur-Glane
491	Santanbien (Henri)	Retired veterinary	29th Marrch 1882, Soissons	Oradour-sur-Glane
492	Santrot (Jules)	Tailor	4th Febuary 1878, Veyrac	Oradour-sur-Glane
493	Santrot (Paul)	Tailor	24th October 1906, Oradour-sur-Glane	Oradour-sur-Glane
494	Mme Gaillot (Cécile), née Saint-Paul	Unemployed	19th January 1904, Montoy-Flanville (Moselle)	Basse-Forêt, Oradour-sur-Glane

	Name	Occupation	Date and place of birth	Residence
495	Mme A. Pister (Victorine), née Sar	Unemployed	10th August 1884, Servigny-Sainte-Barbe	Oradour-sur-Glane
496	Widow Mme Joyeux (Jeanne), née Sathouny	Day labourer	17th June 1874, Sainte-Barbe, Veyrac	Oradour-sur-Glane
497	Mme J. Clavaud (Marie), née Savy	Unemployed	8th September 1882, Oradour-sur-Glane	Le Repaire, Oradour-sur-Glane
498	Sauviat (Paul)	Shoe worker	2nd December 1885, Limoges	15, rue du Mas-Loubier, Limoges
499	Mme Robert (Marguerite), née Senigout	Unemployed	9th March 1878, Saint-Yrieix	La Malaise, Saint-Victurnien
500	Mme Morliéras (Catherine), née Senon	InnKeeper	15th September 1898, Oradour-sur-Glane	Oradour-sur-Glane
501	Senon (Martial)	Lumber-jack	10th November 1886, Oradour-sur-Glane	Oradour-sur-Glane
502	Senon (François)	Farmer	19th April 1866, Oradour-sur-Glane	Oradour-sur-Glane
503	Mme D. Mercier (Jeanne), née Senon	Farmer	5th June 1897, Peyrilhac	Puy-Gaillard, Oradour-sur-Glane
504	Mme P. Vergnaud (Anna), née Senon	Farmer	19th June 1897, Peyrilhac	Oradour-sur-Glane
505	Widow Mme J. Bardet, née Senon	Glover	17th July 1887, Oradour-sur-Glane	"Villa André", Oradour-sur-Glane
506	Senon (Jean)	Farmer	August 1889, Oradour-sur-Glane	Oradour-sur-Glane
507	Senon (Martial)	Roadworker	2nd December 1892, Oradour-sur-Glane	Le Repaire, Oradour-sur-Glane

NUMBER	NAME AND CHRISTIAN NAME	PROFESSION	DATE OF BIRTH	PLACE OF RESIDENCE
508	Widow Mᵐᵉ Rives (Marie), née Senon	Daylabourer	2nd May 1876, Cieux	Oradour-sur-Glane
509	Serano-Pardo (Armonia)		4th June 1941, Limoges	Oradour-sur-Glane
510	Serano-Pardo (Astor-Jean)		8th August 1943, Limoges	Oradour-sur-Glane
511	Serano-Pardo (Paquito-Jacques)		8th August 1943, Limoges	Oradour-sur-Glane
512	Serano-Robles (José)	Teacher	3rd May 1915, Purchera (Espagne)	Oradour-sur-Glane
513	Mᵐᵉ Pinède Robert née Silva (Carmen)	Unemployed	7th August 1904, Bilbao	Oradour-sur-Glane
514	Simon (Marguerite)		20th September 1932, Paris (15ᵉ)	Les Bordes, Oradour-sur-Glane
515	Sirieix (Jean)	Unemployed	25th March 1867, Cieux	Oradour-sur-Glane
516	Mᵐᵉ A. Faure (Marie), née Sudraud	Unemployed	7th August1881, Oradour-sur-Glane	Oradour-sur-Glane
517	Texier (Jean)		5years old, Oradour-sur-Glane	Oradour-sur-Glane
518	Texier (Jean-Camille)		14th january 1916, Saint-Brice	Oradour-sur-Glane
519	Texier (Bernadette)		4years old, Oradour-sur-Glane	Oradour-sur-Glane
520	Texier (Jean)		2years old, Oradour-sur-Glane	Oradour-sur-Glane

521	Texier (Yves)		8 months, Oradour-sur-Glane	Oradour-sur-Glane
522	Mme Thomas (Marie), née Theillaud	InnKeeper	22nd July 1882, Oradour-sur-Glane	Oradour-sur-Glane
523	Mme Brissaud (Marie), née Theillet	Housewife	25th September 1899, Veyrac	Oradour-sur-Glane
524	Thibault (Lucien)		1st December 1932. Pupille de l'Assistance publique	Orbagnac, Oradour-sur-Glane
525	Widow Mme Leroy (Jeanne), née Thieffine	Unemployed	15th September 1882, Gacé (Orne)	La Chatière,Hede (Ille-et-Vilaine)
526	Mme J. Roby (Anna), née Thomas	Farmer	14th November 1885, Oradour-sur-Glane	Le Repaire, Oradour-sur-Glane
527	Thomas (Arthur)		19th January 1934, Veyrac	Lignac, Cieux
528	Mme Vergnaud (Marie), née Thomas	Milliner	6th june 1905, Montceau-les-Mines (Saône-et-Loire)	Oradour-sur-Glane
529	Widow Mme Brun (Catherine), née Thomas	Unemployed	1st Febuary 1881, Cognac-le-Froide	Oradour-sur-Glane
530	Thomas (François)	Unemployed	77 yeears old	Oradour-sur-Glane
531	Mme J. B. Nicolas (Anna), née Thomas	Unemployed	28th March 1892, Saint-Brice-sur-Vienne	Oradour-sur-Glane
532	Widow Mme Texier (Louise), née Thomas	Unemployed	6th December 1893, Saint-Brice-sur-Vienne	Oradour-sur-Glane
533	Thomas (Jean)		25th July 1930, Oradour-sur-Glane	Les Carderies, Oradour-sur-Glane

NUMBER	NAME AND CHRISTIAN NAME	PROFESSION	DATE OF BIRTH	PLACE OF RESIDENCE
534	Thomas (Madeleine)		29th March 1934, Oradour-sur-Glane	Les Carderies, Oradour-sur-Glane
535	Thomas (Anne)		17th December 1939, Oradour-sur-Glane	Les Carderies, Oradour-sur-Glane
536	Mme Raynaud (L.) (Simone), née Thomas	Baker	4th July 1921, La Chapelle-Themer (Vendée)	Oradour-sur-Glane
537	Thomas (Jean)	InnKeeper	70 years old	Oradour-sur-Glane
538	Mme P. Bardet (Catherine), née Thomas	Unemployed	6th January 1908, Oradour-sur-Glane	Oradour-sur-Glane
539	Mme F. Brouillaud (Catherine), née Thomas	Unemployed	15th july 1876, Oradour-sur-Glane	Oradour-sur-Glane
540	Thomas (René)		22nd Febuary 1939, Oradour-sur-Glane	Le Mas du Puy, Oradour-sur-Glane
541	Mme P. Juge (Marie), née Tingaud		27th April 1912, Vitry-sur-Seine (Seine)	Les Brégères, Oradour-sur-Glane
542	Tomasina (Madeleine)	Unemployed	11th April 1936, Paris (6e)	Les Bordes, Oradour-sur-Glane
543	Trouillaud (Roger)	Unemployed	26th August 1916, Argentan (Orne)	Oradour-sur-Glane
544	Trouillaud (Renée)		12th June 1926, Oradour-sur-Glane	Les Bordes, Oradour-sur-Glane

545	Telles (Dominguez-Juan)		14th January 1899, Saragosse (Espagne)	Détaché à Bellac, chez M. Jousset
546	Telles (Philibert-Liberto)		24th August 1942, Limoges	Oradour-sur-Glane
547	Telles (Armonia)		19th October 1936, Barcelone (Espagne)	Oradour-sur-Glane
548	Telles (Miquel)		22nd January 1933, Barcelone (Espagne)	Oradour-sur-Glane
549	Tessaud (Paul)	Accountant	5th July 1922, Saint-Junien	Oradour-sur-Glane
550	Texereau (Josette)		21st May 1936, Oradour-sur-Glane	Oradour-sur-Glane
551	Texereau (Jean)		17th September 1941, Oradour-sur-Glane	Oradour-sur-Glane
552	Texereau (Henri)	Wine Merchant	17th November 1908, Civray (Vienne)	Oradour-sur-Glane
553	Mᵐᵉ J. Lévèque (Mathilde), née Valade	Unemployed	3rd Febuary 1904, Veyrac	Veyrac (Haute-Vienne)
554	Mᵐᵉ J. Couvidou (Germaine), née Valade	Unemployed	6th October 1920, Vaulry	Le Mas-du-Puy, Oradour-sur-Glane
555	Vauchamp (Michèle)		12th June 1937, Oradour-sur-Glane	Les Bordes, Oradour-sur-Glane
556	Mᵐᵉ P. Dupic (Jeanne), née Vergnaud	Unemployed	12th january 1902, Brigueil (Charente)	Oradour-sur-Glane
557	Mᵐᵉ Boulesteix (Léonie), née Vergnaud	Cleaning Woman	30th August 1907, Oradour-sur-Glane	Oradour-sur-Glane

NUMBER	NAME AND CHRISTIAN NAME	PROFESSION	DATE OF BIRTH	PLACE OF RESIDENCE
558	Mme Jean Senon (Maria), née Vergnaud	Farmer	August 1893, Oradour-sur-Glane	Oradour-sur-Glane
559	Vergnaud (François)	Hotelier	9th Febuary 1901, Oradour-sur-Glane	Oradour-sur-Glane
560	Vergnaud (Jean)	Farmer	4th July 1896, Oradour-sur-Glane	Oradour-sur-Glane
561	Mme Picat (Léonie), née Vergnaud	Unemployed	3rd October1891, Oradour-sur-Glane	Oradour-sur-Glane
562	Mme Moreau (Madeleine), née Vevaud	Unemployed	12th October 1888, Saint-Victurnien	Oradour-sur-Glane
563	Vevaud (René)		2nd March 1935, Saint-Brice	Le Mas-du-Puy, Oradour-sur-Glane
564	Vevaud (Gilberte)		9th May 1937, Saint-Brice	Le Mas-du-Puy, Oradour-sur-Glane
565	Mme F. Milord (Juliette), née Vignal	Unemployed	28th July 1919, Oullins	16, rue de la Convention, Oullins
566	Mme Louis Chapaud (Amélie), née Vignaud	Farmer	11th March 1905, Veyrac	L'Ebourliat, Veyrac
567	Mme Jean Pécher (Marguerite), née Vignaud	Unemployedn	3rd September 1911, Limoges	Prinsabaud, Veyrac
568	Vignaud (Marie-Louise)	Domestic	2nd June 1923, Veyrac	Les Brégères, Oradour-sur-Glane
569	Villatte (Christian)		19th March 1944, Limoges	12, rue du Docteur-Bergonié, Limoges
570	Villatte (Pierre)	Tobacconist	22nd September 1889, saint-Gence	Oradour-sur-Glane

N°	Name	Profession	Date and place of birth	Address
571	Villatte (Aimée)	Unemployed	21st December 1915, Saint-Gence	Oradour-sur-Glane
572	Villatte (Amédée)	Controller	9th September 1917, Saint-Gence	12, rue du Docteur-Bergonié, Limoges
573	Mme Ch. Blandin (Marguerite), née Villatte	Unemployed	12th January 1889, Oradour-sur-Glane	Oradour-sur-Glane
574	Villéger (Jean)	Farmer	5th Febuary 1902, Bussière-Bofy	Masset, Oradour-sur-Glane
575	Villéger (Henri)	Farmer	16 years old	Masset, Oradour-sur-Glane
576	Villéger (Guy)	Farmer	8th July 1927, Chamborand (Creuse)	Masset, Oradour-sur-Glane
577	Mme J. Ducharlet (Marie), née Villemonteix	Unemployed	19th December 1864, Javerdat	Oradour-sur-Glane
578	Thomas (Marguerite), née Villemonteix	Domestic	28th october 1919, Cieux	Oradour-sur-Glane
579	Vincent (Jean-Paul)	Teacher	17th August 1942, Limoges	Oradour-sur-Glane
580	Mme Vincent (Raymonde), née Chenet		2nd May 1920, Limoges	Oradour-sur-Glane
580 bis	Mme Gouyon (Annette), née Volozan	Unemployed		19, rue de la Liberté, Limoges
581	Villatte (Pierre)	Unemployed	1st october 1862, Saint-Gence	Oradour-sur-Glane
582	Mme Ramnoux (Albertine), née Zéler	Dressmaker	5th March 1901, Sainte-Marie-aux-Mines (Haut-Rhin)	Oradour-sur-Glane
583	Mme Miozzo (Lucia), née Zoccarato	Farmer	25th July 1904, Campo-de-Saigo (Italie)	Les Brandes, Oradour-sur-Glane

General De Gaulle at Oradour-sur-Glane the 4th June, 1945. At left, Guy Pauchou and at right, Dr. Pierre Masfrand.

Judgement of the civil cour
of Rochechouart, on the 28th May, 1946.

Mme Sophie Garayt, married name Vignal, born on the 25th January, 1880 at Ollières-sur-Eyrieux (department of Ardèche), daughter of Achille and Tinlaud Hermmina, unemployed, residing at Oullières (department of Rhône).

The total number of victims recognized officially-dead is 638 as at the date of going to press.

Some other judgements are pending, which would bring the number of unfortunates that have disappeared to 642.

1st judgement :

Unidentified	585
Identified	52
	637
Added since 1st January, 1946	1
	638
Ending judgement	4
Total	642

Table of contents

Conception et réalisation
Melting Phot
18, boulevard Carnot
87000 Limoges

Achevé d'imprimer en juillet 2003
par les Presses du Centre Imprimerie
1, allée Édouard Le Corbusier
87410 LE PALAIS SUR VIENNE
N° ISBN : 2-910939-08-1
Édition Anglaise : 2-910939-09-X
Dépôt légal : 3ème Trimestre 2003